The NORTHWEST CORNER

For Florien

— Murray Morgan

Also by Murray Morgan

The NORTHWEST CORNER

The Pacific Northwest,
Its Past and Present

Murray Morgan

The Viking Press   *New York*

THIS BOOK IS FOR
EDDIE, ALICE, AND THE UNDINE

First published by The Viking Press, Inc.
625 Madison Avenue, New York 22, N.Y.

Published simultaneously in Canada by
The Macmillan Company of Canada Limited

Library of Congress catalogue card number: 62-11672
Text printed in the U.S.A. by The Murray Printing Co.
Color illustrations printed in the U.S.A. by Civic Printing and Lithographic Corp.
Gravure illustrations printed in Switzerland by Erik Nitsche International

Contents

FOREWORD

COULD IT be that there is no Pacific Northwest?

The thought came as I sought to define the quarter of a million square miles that comprise the northwest corner of the United States and the southwest corner of Canada.

Physically and politically the area exists—Oregon, Washington, Idaho, part of Montana, part of British Columbia—but within this area lying under two flags, such diversity! The rain forests of the Olympic Peninsula, the long reaches of the Strait of Juan de Fuca and Puget Sound, the alpine meadows and frozen peaks of the Cascades; the fir forests of the western slopes, the pines of the eastern; the sweet grasslands of Horse Heaven Hills and the deserts of Central Washington and Oregon, the great bends of the Columbia, cupping the Selkirk Mountains and the oases reclaimed by the Grand Coulee, the sheep country of Idaho and eastern Oregon, the quiet of Crater Lake, the tumult of the Columbia Bar.

Tempered by their surroundings and occupations, the people, too, are diverse. What is the common denominator between the scientist at the Rayonier pulp mill at Shelton studying the spread of radioactive tracers through the cellulose of hemlock and a Basque castrating a sheep in the valley of the Blues? Between the Croatian crewmen of a purse seiner drawing closed their great net in the lee of one of the drowned, sunburned mountaintops of the San Juans and an Indian family knocking apples in the Okanogan? Between a Swedish girl baking cookies in Ballard and the patternman laying out the designs for a missile at Boeing? Between Morris Graves of the mystic painting and Stewart Holbrook of the robust writing? What encompasses the timber cruiser in Oregon, the wheat farmer in the Palouse, the prospector on the Fraser?

An attitude encompasses them—a sense of the newness of their land, a lingering awareness of the isolation once imposed by the mountains to the east and the ocean to the west, a pride in the landscape ("You'd think they were responsible for creation!"), a willingness in work or play to pit themselves against the streams and the mountains, the forest and the ocean.

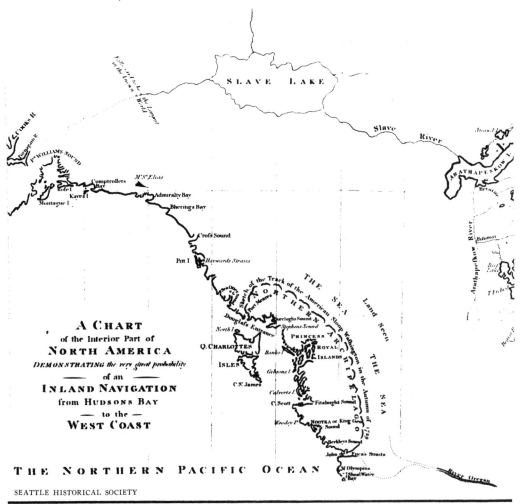

SEATTLE HISTORICAL SOCIETY

OPPOSITE: *The Needles at Cannon Beach, Oregon.*

RAY ATKESON

Storm approaching at Crescent Beach, Oregon.

10

The Oregon Coast Highway, one of the most spectacular in the world, clings to the cliff edge of the continent and presents the traveler with vistas of headlands thrusting into the ocean along with close-ups of the waves smashing white against the dark rocks.

The OCEAN
......*then*

THE LAND lay hidden behind the ocean that was both highway and shield. The Spaniards had taken over the empire of the Aztecs and Toltecs, but their energy was directed toward finding gold and breaking the conquered Indians to harness. They probed California and drew back, their curiosity not encompassing the Northwest Coast. The empty sea continued to pulse against an all but empty land.

In 1579 the *Golden Hind,* under the zealous Francis Drake, came raiding along the coast of South America and up past Mexico, plundering cities and ships before it disappeared into the northern mists, presumably headed for the Northwest Passage that was said to lead back through the continent to the Atlantic. We do not know for sure how far north Drake sailed, only that he approached the southern extremity of what is now considered the Pacific Northwest. He wrote the first complaints about our weather, noting "most vile, thicke and stinking fogges," which may have reminded him of home, for he called the country New Albion. Finally Drake gave up his search for a shortcut, crossed the Pacific, and sailed west to England, having decided "there is no passage at all through these Northerne coasts . . . or if there be, yet it is unnavigable."

The Spaniards were not so sure. The *Golden Hind,* appearing from nowhere, disappearing into the unknown, aroused them somewhat to the danger inherent in their ignorance of the coastline to the north. An expedition was organized and dispatched, though hardly with vigor; twenty years slipped by between the time of Drake's raid and the explorers' departure, and then they were put under the command of Sebastián Vizcaíno, a merchant described by one chronicler as "devoid of executive ability and not overburdened with courage." However, one of Vizcaíno's subalterns, Martin Aguilar, may have taken the tiny ship *Tres Reyes* as far north as the mouth of the Rogue in southern Oregon.

The defeat of the Armada had drained Spanish energy. The Jesuits and Franciscans continued to remind Spain of the need for further exploration, but the distant court felt no urgency. In the wry words of the historian Bancroft, "Many times was the King reminded of the rich spiritual harvest to be gathered in California by friars who never allowed him to forget the secular advantages to be gained by complying with their wishes." But neither the prospect of new souls nor that of more gold aroused the monarch. Exploration was forgotten until something new appeared in the north: the Russians.

In 1741 Vitus Bering led a Russian scientific expedition across the North Pacific to the Alaskan mainland. He was shipwrecked on the return voyage and died of scurvy on the Komandorskie Islands. Survivors of the Bering party pieced together a small boat from the wreckage of their vessel and managed to sail back to Kamchatka. They arrived clad in the pelts of sea otters, a delightful animal with lustrous fur that became more coveted than sable, worth more than its weight in gold. In pursuit of the otter, the Russians established bases along the Aleutians, along the Alaska Peninsula, down the mainland shore toward Mexico.

Alarmed again, and rightly, the Spaniards moved to occupy the land they claimed. They built missions and presidios in Upper California, made Monterey their capital, founded San Francisco to guard the approaches. In 1774 the viceroy dispatched a new party of exploration in the vessel *Santiago,* again choosing for leader a not particularly vigorous captain, Juan Josef Pérez Hernández. He sailed north to 55 degrees, somehow managing to avoid landfalls, but on his return voyage touched on the west coast of Vancouver Island, anchoring in a roadstead of twenty-five fathoms. Presumably this was the sound we still know by its Indian name, Nootka. Pérez called it San Lorenzo.

The fogs of time conceal the details of that first confrontation of the white men of Western Europe with the Indians of the Northwest Coast, but from the records of subsequent meetings it is not hard to imagine the scene: the gray beach; the low bank on which stood the long houses of split cedar boards, their doorways fantastically painted; the dark evergreen forest rising to the mountains; the little ship with its great flag; the Spanish officers in rich uniform; the swarthy seamen, unshaven, rotting with scurvy, uneasily turning the swivel guns as the first small dugouts put out from shore, approached, drew off, approached again; then the ceremonial march of the chief to the water line to take his seat in the enormous, high-prowed war canoe; the chant of the wildly painted paddlers mingling with the cries of the wheeling gulls; the women in skirts made from the inner fluff of cedar bark spreading feathers on the green waters; the ultimate meeting on the *Santiago*'s deck of the representatives of two stiff, formal, successive civilizations.

The Indians of the Northwest Coast—the Tlingit, the Haida, the Chimmesyan, the Kwakiutl, the Bella Coola, the Salish, and the Chinook—had admirably adapted their life to their ocean-shore environment. Not yet in the iron age, with no agriculture to speak of, they wrested their food from the sea (even venturing beyond sight of land to kill whales), their shelter from the forest (which supplied not only boards for houses and fuel for fires but even shredded bark for skirts and rain capes, and roots that could be woven into hats). After hunting and gathering, they had time and energy to develop a powerful art form in which men, animals, and gods were mingled in strange and intricate carvings. These Indians were perhaps the most gifted whittlers of all time.

Theirs was an economy of abundance, so overflowing that they invented the ceremony of the potlatch as a means of investing surplus. At a potlatch an Indian who had accumulated wealth gave it away, knowing that custom decreed that any recipient who failed to repay his offering with interest lost prestige. In time the potlatch degenerated into a competition between the richest to see who could afford to waste the most treasure by burning it: a symbolic armaments race.

They had furs to spare, the Indians of the Northwest Coast. But Pérez was a military man, not a merchant. He was unimpressed by the fact that the leading men of the tribe wore robes of sea otter worthy of a princess's ransom. If there was trading, it was slight; Pérez sailed south to San Blas to report land deserving further investigation.

The Spaniards were back the next year to investigate. They came in two vessels, the frigate *Santiago* again, this time commanded by Don Bruno Hezeta (Heceta), and the little schooner *Sonora,* under a charming young officer with the elaborate name of Francisco de la Bodega y Quadra.

Not long after daybreak on the morning of July 14, 1775, the two vessels lay rolling quietly at anchor off the southern coast of the Olympic Peninsula. This is the one time of year when the weather is almost certain to be fair; on such mornings the heads of the Olympics stand improbably white and high over the shouldering ranges matted with rain forest. The wind must have been light that morning, for both the *Santiago* and the *Sonora* saw fit to dispatch landing parties through the breakers—a morning, probably, of heavy swells unflecked with white until they broke evenly on the dark sands.

Hezeta led a party made up of his priest, his pilot, his surgeon, and twenty armed men to take possession of the land for Christ and the Crown, while Bodega y Quadra, a league to the south, sent his boatswain and a half dozen seamen to fill casks with fresh water. Most scholars now think that the ceremonial marriage of the land to Castille took place on the lovely curved beach just south of Point Grenville, though a few still argue for a point farther north. Whatever the exact spot, the taking of possession went well, the Spaniards being adept at ceremonials. Hezeta called the place "Rada de Bucareli."

The fetching of fresh water proved to be another matter. As the party under Boatswain Pedro Santa Ana approached the mouth of the Moclips, they were ambushed by Indians who had concealed themselves in the tidewrack of the beach and the undergrowth on the bank. Not a Spaniard escaped. Not even the name that Hezeta fixed on Point Grenville—Punta de los Martires—survived, though it is argued that the name eventually given to Destruction Island may be a misplaced tribute to the fallen Spaniards.

The loss of the landing party crippled the expedition, which accomplished little more on that voyage. On his way back to Mexico, Hezeta detected signs of the outflow of a great river, presumably the Columbia, which he named, sight unseen, the San Roque. With his crew short-handed and scurvy-raddled, Hezeta did not try to cross the bar. Considering his luck, it was just as well.

Of these first Spanish voyages the world heard little. Not so the visit of the next explorer, Captain James Cook. That great man, most painstaking of explorers, was on his third and last voyage, his mission being no less than the discovery of the long-sought Northwest Passage.

As exploration, Cook's performance on the Northwest Coast in March and April 1779 was several cuts below his prime standard. He failed to find and probe either the Columbia or the Strait of Juan de Fuca, each of which merited investi-

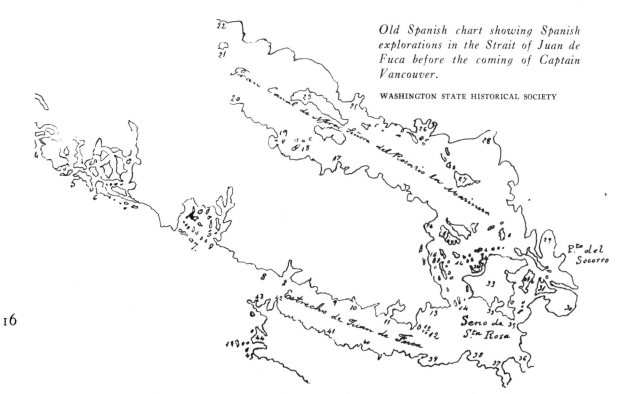

Old Spanish chart showing Spanish explorations in the Strait of Juan de Fuca before the coming of Captain Vancouver.

WASHINGTON STATE HISTORICAL SOCIETY

16

gation as a possible gateway east. Eventually he put into Nootka, where he spent a month repairing his two ships, the *Resolution* and the *Discovery*.

With Cook on that voyage was the first American to see the far side of his continental homeland, a foot-loose, wind-blown man of twenty-seven years named John Ledyard. He had run away from Dartmouth College (by canoe) and knocked about the Atlantic and the Mediterranean until, finding himself stranded in England just before the Revolutionary War, he signed on for the Cook expedition. Now, encountering the Indians of Nootka, he noted that they were "the same kind of people that inhabit the opposite side of the continent," a sentiment with which his commander agreed. When the inhabitants failed to charge him for fuel and water, Cook remarked, "These are Americans indeed." Corporal Ledyard was stirred by the thought that Nootka was the back door to home. "Though more than 2000 miles distant from the nearest part of New England," he wrote, underestimating the distance considerably, "I felt myself plainly affected. It soothed a homesick heart and rendered me very tolerably happy."

While Cook's vessels were being worked over, a brisk barter was carried on between crew and tribesmen. The Indians were wild for metal. In exchange for buttons and bits of iron, cup hooks, and the knobs and hinges off chests, they offered fish, venison, slave girls, wooden masks, bags of ocher and roasted human arms and hands. (Corporal Ledyard, a man of experimental bent, tried the latter delicacy but confessed that "either my conscience or my taste rendered it very odious to me." Most sought after by the crew were furs, partly because the ships were headed north into the Arctic, partly because they felt the furs would be useful for trade in Atlantic ports. The Indians offered skins of bears, wolves, foxes, deer, racoons, skunks, martens, and—most prized—sea otters. Most of the otter skins available at Nootka were in poor condition, since on cold days the Indians wore them fishing, and from time to time draped them over pots of boiling food to steam out the vermin, which they ate.

Nor did the crew treat the sea-otter skins as valuables. When the ships sailed into the Arctic that summer in a vain attempt to push across the roof of North America to the Atlantic, the men used the furs as bedding. While in the Sandwich Islands (where Cook was killed in a skirmish with the natives) they stuffed the pelts in seabags and left them to molder in the tropic damp. In Kamchatka, where otter skins were not uncommon, they gave a few away. Then, homeward bound in 1780, they put into Macao. While the ships were taking on supplies at the Great Quay under the rocky hills of the Portuguese town, Lieutenant James King received permission to go by a Chinese boat up the bay to the walled and forbidden city of Canton. He took with him twenty otter skins to see what they might fetch from members of the *hong,* the exclusive trading class.

The Chinese merchants were enchanted. China's only supply of sea-otter furs came from the Russians, who delivered them at a remote Siberian border village to be freighted south by caravan. The merchants offered King forty dollars each for his twenty tattered skins and asked for more. There were more on the ships at Macao, the lieutenant said. Let's go, said the Chinese.

In Macao, King wrote in his journal:

> We found that during our absence a brisk trade had been carrying on with the Chinese for the sea-otter skins which had every day been rising in their value. One of our seamen sold his stock alone for eight hundred dollars; and a few prime skins which were clean and had been well preserved were sold for one hundred and twenty dollars each. . . . When it is remembered that the furs were at first collected without our having any idea of their real value; that the greatest part of them had been worn by the Indians, from whom we purchased them; that they were afterwards preserved with little care, and frequently used for bed-clothes and other purposes, during our cruise to the north; and that, probably, we had never got the full value for them in China, the advantages that might be derived from a voyage to that part of the American coast, undertaken with commercial views, appear to me of a degree of importance sufficient to call for the attention of the public.

So, too, it appeared to John Ledyard. The dream of sea trade with northwest America, and of possible overland trading routes, smoldered in him. But British merchants of 1780 were not anxious to risk voyages to the North Pacific when American and French privateers were at large, nor was a corporal of Colonial antecedents exactly the man to approach them.

In the closing days of the War of the American Revolution, however, Ledyard was shipped home to fight against his native land. He promptly deserted. Finding refuge in his uncle's Connecticut law offices, Ledyard wrote an account of his experiences in the North Pacific five years earlier. He exhorted his fellow Americans to beat the British to the fur coast. But it was already too late.

In 1785 an obscure British trader named James Hanna, having heard stories in China of the wealth of furs available on the Northwest Coast, crossed the Pacific in a tiny, sixty-ton brig and swapped trinkets with the natives for 560 sea-otter skins, which he sold in Macao that September for $20,600. Hanna invested his profit in a new boat, appropriately named *Sea Otter,* which he sailed to the coast the following year, only to find that two East India Company ships out of Bombay, the *Captain Cook* and the *Experiment,* commanded by Captain James Strange, had been in the vicinity a few weeks earlier, and had left with 600 of the prime pelts.

Traffic was soon congested on the fur routes. That same year the Comte de La Pérouse, France's most able navigator, cruised the shoreline in vain search of the Northwest Passage. Stopping at Monterey in September, the Frenchmen mentioned to the Spaniards that the Russians in Alaska were pushing their outposts south. This rumor, along with independent evidence that Englishmen were prowling the northern preserve, impelled the Spaniards into motion, though slowly; their response to the challenge was so tinged with *mañana* that two years passed before they sent an expedition to the Gulf of Alaska to see what the Russians were up to. The envoys found the Russian still busy consolidating their grip on Alaska, but brought back word that the English were thick as sandfleas on the beaches between California and Alaska.

The tide of English sea peddlers was rising toward flood, and it carried to the Northwest Coast some memorable adventurers. Among them were Lieutenant Nathaniel Portlock and Captain George Dixon, who had both been with Cook, and who returned under a license granted by the King George's Sound Company. There was Captain Charles W. Barkley, who brought his seventeen-year-old wife Frances, the first white woman to gaze on this part of the world (and quite a sight herself to the Indians). There was Captain John Meares, a tough, devious ex-lieutenant in the British navy, who lost over half of his men to scurvy on his first visit but came back in 1788 with two vessels under the convenient flag of Portugal, a stratagem which he employed to avoid conflict with the East India and South Seas Companies' monopoly rights, but which was to play its part in the serio-comic melodrama of the Nootka controversy.

Thinking of the great emptiness of the Northwest Coast at that time, when there were no white settlements between the little Spanish outpost at San Francisco and the Russian fur-trading camps on Cook Inlet, one easily forgets the frequency with which the peddlers and explorers fell in with each other in the fir-girt harbors between. Such encounters were frequent enough to make the lonely men, half a world from home, often sick and needing supplies, more likely to resent than welcome the sight of a rival sail. It was at Nootka that the rasp and abrasion of these encounters finally wore through the amenities of civilized intercourse.

The year was 1789, and the actor with the loudest role was inevitably John Meares, who had expanded his operations to include five ships. Meares was using Nootka as his base for trading up and down the coast; he had brought over a number of Chinese from Macao to perform skilled labor; he had—so he said later—given Chief Maquinna two pistols in exchange for land at Nootka, on which he built a rude compound enclosing a workshop in front of which he mounted a three-pound gun on a swivel. With the help of the tribesmen, who were paid in trinkets each evening at the ringing of a bell, his men had assembled and launched a little sloop, the *North West America,* the first ship built on the coast. (He forgot to tether it at the launching and it started out to sea on the outgoing tide.) Meares planned a permanent settlement at Nootka, but in those first years his ships wintered either in the Sandwich Islands or back in Macao.

In the spring of 1789 the Viceroy of Mexico dispatched a colonizing expedition to occupy Nootka. The party was led by Captain Estaban José Martínez and it included priests for converting the Indians, workmen to build a garrison, soldiers to man it, and instructions "to prevent as far as possible [foreign] intercourse and commerce with the natives." But when his ship, the twenty-six gun *Princessa,* rounded Breaker Point and put into Friendly Harbor at Nootka on May 3, Martínez was greeted in English.

In port was one of Meares' vessels, the *Iphigenia,* with her questionable Portugese papers and her indubitably English skipper, William Douglas. Also present were two vessels flying the unfamiliar flag of the United States of America, of which George Washington had been inaugurated as first President only a week before. These Boston vessels, the first Americans in the eastern Pacific, were the stocky, broad-beamed, double-decked *Columbia Rediviva,* and her consort, the ninety-ton sloop *Lady Washington.* They were belated fruit borne of John Ledyard's propaganda on behalf of American commerce with the Indians of the fur coast. They had come the year before and had wintered at Nootka.

The *Lady Washington,* under the energetic Robert Gray, was just putting to sea on a trading run north when Martínez arrived. Gray paused only long enough to trade courtesies and drinks with the Spaniard; but Captain John Kendrick on the *Columbia,* an oddly procrastinating type to have achieved command of a Yankee trader, welcomed another excuse to remain at anchor. Thus Kendrick was witness to events that threatened Europe with war.

In the situation which found together a Spanish warship, an American merchantman, and an English vessel displaying the Portuguese flag, in a harbor of disputed nationality, the Americans and the Spanish were natural allies. Kendrick had sailed against the English during the Revolutionary War; Spain and England were at loggerheads. So when Martínez decided that the *Iphigenia* was sailing under false colors and ordered her seized and her officers arrested, Kendrick was an amused onlooker. When Martínez relented and released Douglas but ordered him to be gone to China, Kendrick witnessed the bond Douglas was forced to sign for the value of his vessel.

Kendrick was still at hand when another of Meares' vessels, the home-made *North West America,* put in at Nootka and was seized by the Spanish ostensibly as security for supplies furnished the *Iphigenia.* The Spanish rechristened her the *Gertrudis,* and Kendrick loaned Martínez one of his American officers, David Coolidge, to sail the *Gertrudis* on a trading voyage.

There now arrived another of Meares' vessels, the *Princess Royal,* captained by Thomas Hudson, and shortly afterward the *Lady Washington* returned from a discouraging search for otter skins. Martínez availed himself of this international assemblage to stage a formal act of possession. After the priests and soldiery made suitable religious and military demonstrations, Martínez stood on

A mother sea otter holding her helpless pup. The abundance of sea otters along the Northwest Coast and the lure of their valuable pelts, most prized fur in the world, brought white men in large numbers to the area in the late 1700s. Except for small groups off the Monterey Peninsula and among the Aleutians, the otter herds were exterminated. Now under strict government protection, the sea otters are making a comeback.

Nootka Sound on the west coast of Vancouver Island became a center of the sea-otter trade and the focal point of controversy between England and Spain over title to the area. Here is the Indian village as seen by an artist accompanying the Vancouver expedition in 1792.

The first vessel launched on the Northwest Coast hit the water at Nootka Sound on September 20, 1788. She was built by Chinese laborers brought by Captain Meares from Macao for the purpose. Here is the launching of the North West America *as depicted in Meares'* Voyages . . . to the Northwest Coast of America, *published in London in 1790. The sloop in the background flying the American flag is the* Lady Washington, *Captain Robert Gray.*

This portrait is generally considered to be of Captain George Vancouver, though the National Gallery in London cannot trace its history further back than a sale in 1878. The chart of North America's west coast on the globe tends to identify the painting with Vancouver, as does the goiter, but it was unusual for a naval officer to be portrayed in mufti.

the beach with drawn sword and intoned on behalf of Spain, "I take, and I have taken, I seize and I have seized, possession of this soil . . . for all time to come." The Indians also watched.

The *Princess Royal* was allowed to depart unhindered, but when the *Argonaut,* yet another of Meares' ships, showed up carrying a prefabricated warehouse, the frame of a schooner, and more Chinese laborers, Martínez managed to provoke a quarrel with her master, Captain James Colnett (explaining later that he had picked up enough English from the Americans to understand the phrase "Goddamned Spaniard") and seized her. When the *Princess Royal* returned, she too was impounded. Martínez dispatched both ships, with their officers imprisoned, to San Blas. In time the Viceroy of Mexico freed them.

The bemused Kendrick found the Northwest Coast and its operatic events too fascinating to forsake. When the Spanish commander offered to pay in otter pelts if the Americans would take the English sailors left over from the *North West Coast* back to China, Kendrick transferred himself to the little *Lady Washington* and ordered Gray to sail the larger *Columbia* back to New England by way of Canton. Thus Kendrick lost the honor of being the first American to carry the flag around the world, but he gained a ship, for he never did return to Boston with the sloop, or, for that matter, pay for her.

Gray carried out his assignment. Cannon saluted the *Columbia Rediviva* when she sailed into Boston harbor. Though the first trip to the fur coast had not produced the expected profit, the owners sent Gray back almost immediately with the frame of a schooner and a stock of trading goods that included 14,000 nails, 143 sheets of copper, 4000 chisels, and racks of war-surplus blunderbusses and muskets.

Meanwhile the Nootka dispute had blossomed into a full-blown international crisis. The quarrels of the English and Spanish captains in Friendly Harbor on the backside of an island off the far coast of America, as judged in London and Madrid from the one-sided reports of those involved, were symbols of aggressive intent. The governments exchanged sharp notes. The Spanish claimed Nootka by the right of discovery and papal award; the British rejected the argument and demanded redress for the seizures. Spain ordered mobilization of its navy. At this stage, who should show up in London but Meares himself; he submitted a memorial to the House of Commons claiming that the Spaniards had deprived him, a veteran of His Majesty's Navy, of 153,000 Spanish dollars and had prevented his earning another half million. Commons approved King George's order to impress enough seamen to put the Royal Navy on war footing. Holland and Prussia lined up behind England. Spain sought the support of France but failed to get it, since Louis XVI was facing revolution at home. So, her bluff called, Spain backed down and agreed to the Nootka Convention, under which the Spaniards promised to restore the property Martínez had seized (the officers and men had already been freed) and to agree that nationals of both Spain and England would not be disturbed in carrying out trade with the natives in the Pacific. The British made the minor concession of agreeing not to trade illicitly with the established Spanish settlements south of Nootka.

Captain George Vancouver, an able though somewhat morose officer who had been on the Northwest Coast with Cook, was dispatched to Nootka to receive formal restitution from the Spanish. He was also instructed to survey the coast from latitude 30 north to Cook Inlet in Alaska—a final search for the Northwest Passage. Renewed interest in that legendary shortcut had been incited by Meares' printed account of his voyages, Meares having intimated that the American Robert Gray had found Nootka to be on an island and that the Strait of Juan de Fuca opened onto a passage that might lead almost to Hudson Bay.

So it was that both Gray and Vancouver were on the Northwest Coast in the spring of 1792, Gray trading and Vancouver exploring. They sighted each other off the Olympic Peninsula on April 28. John Boit, the eighteen-year-old fifth mate on the *Columbia*, recorded the meeting in his journal:

> This day spoke his Britannic Majesty's ships *Discovery* and *Chatham,* commanded by Captain George Vancouver and Lieutenant William Broughton, from England, on a voyage of discovery. . . . A boat boarded us from the *Discovery* and we gave them all the information we had especially about the Strait of Juan de Fuca, which they were in search of. They bore away for the strait's mouth which was not far distant.

The officers from the *Discovery* who boarded the *Columbia* were Peter Puget and Archibald Menzies. They told Gray of the discovery Meares had credited him with. Gray disavowed it, explaining that he had entered the Strait of Juan de Fuca in 1789 in the *Lady Washington* but had turned back after sailing about fifty miles and re-entered the ocean by the same route. "Mr. Meares must have trusted to bad Information in that respect," Puget wrote in his journal, while Menzies commented acerbly that Meares' yarn was "a fallacy which no excuse can justify."

On leaving Gray, Vancouver entered the Strait of Juan de Fuca, which most likely had been first seen in 1787 by Captain Barkley (he with the seventeen-year-old bride aboard the *Imperial Eagle*) and which had been charted by the Spaniards Alferez Manuel Quimper and Francisco Eliza in 1790 and 1791. Vancouver pursued the strait east, then turned south into the inland sea of Puget Sound. Though it disappointingly proved to be a dead end, providing no passage to the Atlantic, Vancouver was enchanted with the sea in the forest. He wrote in his journal:

> The serenity of the climate, the innumerable pleasing landscapes, and the abundant fertility that unassisted nature puts forth, require only to be enriched by the industry of man with villages, mansions, cottages and other buildings, to render it the most lovely country that can be imagined; whilst the labour of the inhabitants would be amply rewarded, in the bounties which nature seems ready to bestow on cultivation.

Departing the sound, Vancouver circumnavigated Vancouver Island (nearly losing the *Discovery* on a ledge on the approach to Queen Charlotte Sound) and put in at Nootka.

Meanwhile Captain Gray in the *Columbia* had been cruising south along the Olympic peninsula. He discovered Gray's Harbor, where there were both trading and fighting with the Indians, who made the mistake of attempting to approach the *Columbia* at night in their canoes. "One large canoe with at least 20 men in her got within ½ pistol shot of the quarter," wrote young Boit. "With a nine pounder loaded with langrage and about 10 muskets loaded with buckshot, we dashed her all to pieces."

The next day Gray, in his own words, "sent up the main top gallant yard and set all sail." Gray sailed south to make the most important single discovery credited to an American sea captain, the Columbia River.

At four o'clock on the morning of May 10, he noted, "Saw the entrance of our desired port." For four hours he stood off the bar of the great river, then, "at 8 a.m. being a little to the windward of the entrance of the harbor, bore away, and run in east-northeast, between the breakers, having from five to seven fathoms of water. When we were over the bar we found this to be a large river of fresh water, up which we steered. Many canoes came alongside. At 1 p.m. came to with the small bower, in two fathoms, black and white sand. The entrance between the bars bore west-southwest, distant ten miles. The north side of the river a half-mile distant from the ship; the south side of the same, two and a half miles distance; a village on the north side of the river west by north, distance three quarters of a mile. Vast numbers of natives came alongside. People employed pumping salt water out of our water casks, in order to fill with fresh, while the ship float in. So ends."

So ended the period of ocean exploration. The coast was known, the existence of a usable Northwest Passage was all but disproved. The land was there to be used and developed. The protecting shield of the ocean was now but a roadway.

The Oregon Coast
PHOTOS: OPPOSITE: JOHSEL NAMKUNG;
PAGES 30-31: ELIOT ELISOFON

The OCEAN
...... *now*

THE SHORELINE of the Northwest Coast remains much as the explorers saw it: wave-carved and wind-scoured, with narrow beaches of sand snuggled between the outthrust rocks; a reach, beautiful but wild; above all, remote, solitary.

No large cities stand on the shore of the open ocean. The few towns that have taken root on that exposed coast, like the trees that take the first shock of the five-thousand-mile sweep of wind, are tough and tenacious, but small. Behind the bars guarding the bays and rivers, or beside the protected inland seas, well back from the Pacific, the great cities grow. Most of the miles of the shoreline remain the homeland of Indians, the playground of whites.

To those of us who live in the Northwest, the ocean shore is a retreat, a place to visit in search of fish and clams or beauty and isolation.

When we go to the shore we revisit our childhood, and that of mankind.

Columbia River Gorge.

The RIVERS
......then

THE STREAMS that rise in the coastal mountains and fall into the western sea are steep, turbulent, short, and—except to those who live beside them, or cherish the salmon and the trout—unimportant. Their names, though fascinating, are little known: the Skeena, the Bella Coola, and the Klinaklini; the Hoh, the Queets, the Quinault, and the Moclips; the Willapa and the Nasella; the Nahelem, the Nesticca, and the Umpqua. But two majestic streams rise far behind the coastal ranges, in the great snowfields and glaciers that cling to the spine of the continent; they gather their waters from an area larger than France and Germany, and burst through the mountain barricades to find the sea. These rivers, the Fraser and the Columbia, have carved into our history paths as deep as those they cut from the shining mountains to the western sea.

In the year that Captain Gray steered his little trading vessel across what a later captain called "the bare ribs of the continent, that seven-shoaled horror, the Columbia River bar," giving the United States its decisive claim to the Oregon country, one of the last of the Spanish explorers in the North Pacific, José María Narváez, knocking about the Strait of Georgia in the leaky schooner *Santa*

Saturnia, detected the milky residue of a great river pouring down from the mountains. He did not try to explore it but named it Boca de Florida Blanca. Vancouver, passing that way soon after, missed in the fog even the signs of the stream, an oversight not as important to history as his bypassing the Columbia. The more northern of the great rivers was to be discovered by other sons of the empire soon enough. As the pursuit of sea-otter pelts had led the American Robert Gray around the Horn to the incidental discovery of the mouth of the Columbia, the hunt for the beaver skin was to lead two of history's more stubborn Scotsmen, Alexander Mackenzie and Simon Fraser, down the more northerly of the great rivers to the ocean.

During the winter Vancouver spent at Nootka working out with the Spanish commander the details of joint occupation of the Northwest Coast, Alexander Mackenzie, then twenty-five years old and already a partner in the North West Company, was wintering on the upper Peace River on the eastern slopes of the Rockies. Mackenzie dreamed of finding a practical trade route across the continent—an overland Northwest Passage. Already he had discovered and followed to its mouth the north-flowing Mackenzie, a feat his single-minded associates considered valueless since the stream emptied not into the Pacific with its sea otters but into the tundra wastes of the Arctic. Now Mackenzie was planning to try again for the Pacific. "I send you a couple of guineas," he wrote his cousin on departure. "The rest I take with me to traffic with the Russians."

When the ice broke in the spring of 1793, Mackenzie and a nine-man party of Indian and French-Canadian *voyageurs* climbed into their big canoe, "twenty-five feet long within," he noted proudly, and, seated atop a ton and a half of baggage, began the tedious upstream passage. When they could they paddled; when paddling was impossible, they towed the canoe; when the river was impassable, they portaged. The little party fought its way up the Peace to the Parsnip, up the Parsnip until it became too shallow and tortuous for the big canoe. Indians told them of a portage; they carried the canoe 817 paces over a ridge to a mountain lake, which drained westward.

Now they were on a tributary of the North Fork of the Fraser, a stream that Fraser himself—most literal of men—was to christen the Bad River. And bad it was. On their first day going downstream the party was caught in white water that swamped the canoe; they saved it, but lost half their ammunition. Mackenzie followed the Fraser around the Big Bend, where it skirts the northern abutment of the Cariboos and turns south through the wild waters of Fort George Canyon. In his journal Mackenzie was less impressed by the wild waters of the canyon than by the wild onions growing on the river bank, noting that these so added to the tastiness of their pemmican as to make everyone very hungry, "rather inconvenient to the state of our provisions."

Worried that the river continued south rather than west, Mackenzie consulted some Indians. In the great tradition of persons living beside rivers they warned the canoeists of impassable rapids ahead. The Scot was no man to fear white water but he did worry about time and distance. If this was indeed the great River of the West, he feared the trip to the ocean would be too long for him to be able to complete it and return across the mountains that year; he was too short of provisions and ammunition to winter on the coast. So, persuading his men to abandon their much-patched canoe, he led them away from the river and westward over an almost imperceptible Indian trail to the Bella Coola, down which, having traded with the Indians for a dugout, they paddled to the ocean.

On a rock fronting the sea, the first man to cross the continent by land north of Mexico painted "in large characters" a message in red ocher mixed with bear's grease:

> Alexander Mackenzie, from Canada, by land, the twenty-second of
> July, one thousand seven hundred and ninety-three. Lat. 52° 20′ 48″ N.

Then Mackenzie and his party fought their way back over the mountains and reached Fort Chipewyan on the Peace in late September after a paddle and march of 134 days. "Here my voyages of discovery terminate," he wrote. "Their toils and their dangers, their solicitudes and sufferings, have not been exaggerated. On the contrary, in many instances language has failed me in the attempt to describe them."

In his *Voyages* Mackenzie outlined a plan for extending the British fur trade "to the markets of the four quarters of the globe" but fifteen years were to pass before another Scot, the bullet-headed, indomitable Simon Fraser, born in Vermont of loyalist parents, received permission from his partners in the North West Company to try to follow to the sea the river Mackenzie had discovered, which was still suspected to be the Columbia.

No man has ever been more matter of fact than Fraser. In the journal that all North West Company men were obliged to keep, he noted on May 22, 1808, "Having made every necessary preparation for a long voyage, we embarked at five o'clock a.m." So began one of the great river voyages. Fraser described his journal as "exceedingly ill wrote worse worded and not well spelt," but even as tidied up by editors its account of the descent of that wild river reverberates with the splash and thump of danger, the pain of starvation that reduced the party to eating dog meat discarded by the Indians, the dread moments when the men found themselves trapped in a canyon too precipitous for portaging with no choice but "to embark as it were a corps perdu upon the mercy of this awful tide." But finally they had to forsake the canoes and scramble along the banks of the stream, at times trusting their lives to the firmness of clumps of moss.

"I have been for a long period among the Rocky Mountains," Fraser wrote, "but have never seen anything like this country. We had to pass where no human being should venture; yet in those places there is a regular footpath impressed, or rather indented upon the very rocks by frequent travelling. Besides this, steps which are formed like a ladder or the shrouds of a ship, by poles hanging to one another and crossed at certain distances with twigs, the whole suspended from the top to the foot of immense precipices and fastened at both extremities to stones and trees, furnish a safe and convenient passage to the Natives; but we, who have not had the advantage of their education and experience, were often in imminent danger when obliged to follow their example."

They fought their way through and reached the tidal river. They traded with the Indians for dugouts and as they paddled gazed in wonder at "cedars five fathoms in circumference and proportionate height." But before they reached open water they found themselves under attack by the surly Cowichan Indians. Reluctantly Fraser turned back. A check of the latitude had convinced him that his hardships had been endured in pursuit of an illusion: "The latitude is 49 degrees nearly, while that of the entrance of the Columbia is 46° 20'," he noted flatly in his journal. "This river is therefore not the Columbia."

Nor was it, obviously, an easy path for fur traders seeking a route to the Pacific. Nature's true highway lay to the south, as Fraser may have suspected when, outbound, he had heard from Indians tales of a party of white men who had not many years before him descended "the other river." That party had been the forty-three-man Corps of Discovery under Meriwether Lewis and William Clark following the Columbia to the sea.

The corps, which in spite of its celebrated hardships had things a good deal easier than Fraser's famished contingent, had been activated by the same forces that put the Scot and his companions on the wrong river: Mackenzie's demonstration that an overland passage was possible; the dreams of tying together the continental beaver business and the coastal sea-otter trade; an appreciation that control of the mysterious Columbia was vital to domination of the Northwest Coast.

Long before he had become President of the United States, Thomas Jefferson had encountered in Paris that rollingest of unmossed stones, John Ledyard, and had encouraged him in a fantastic project that Ledyard actually undertook: to walk across Europe and Siberia, hitchike the Pacific in a fur trader's boat, then continue his walk across the continent to New England. It had not worked out (Ledyard got as far as central Siberia before being arrested and sent packing by the Czar's secret police; now he lay dead in, of all places, Egypt) but Jefferson's intellectual curiosity about the unmapped West had, with the purchase of the

Dear Sir

Washington. US. of America. July 4. 1803.

In the journey which you are about to undertake for the discovery of the course and source of the Missisipi, and of the most convenient water communication from thence to the Pacific ocean, your party being small, it is to be expected that you will encounter considerable dangers from the Indian inhabitants. should you escape those dangers and reach the Pacific ocean, you may find it imprudent to hazard a return the same way, and be forced to seek a passage round by sea in such vessels as you may find on the Western coast. but you will be without money, without clothes, & other necessaries; as a sufficient supply cannot be carried with you from hence. your resource in that case can only be in the credit of the US. for which purpose I hereby authorise you to draw on the Secretaries of State, of the Treasury, of War & of the Navy of the US. according as you may find your draughts will be most negociable, for the purpose of obtaining money or necessaries for yourself & your men: and I solemnly pledge the faith of the United States that these draughts shall be paid punctually at the date they are made payable. I also ask of the Consuls, agents, merchants & citizens of any nation with which we have intercourse or amity to furnish you with those sup-plies which your necessities may call for, assuring them of honorable and prompt retribution. and our own Consuls in foreign parts where you may happen to be, are hereby instructed & required to be aiding & assisting to you in whatsoever may be necessary for procuring your return back to the United States. And to give more entire satisfaction & confidence to those who may be disposed to aid you, I Thomas Jefferson, President of the United States of America, have written this letter of general credit for you with my own hand, and signed it with my name.

Th: Jefferson

To
Capt. Meriwether Lewis.

Louisiana Territory, been turned into a national need to know. Word that the North West Company's talented traders were crossing the Rockies and that one had reached the Pacific hardened the President's determination to hurl an American expedition into the western unknown. And his was the power.

On May 14, 1804, the government explorers departed St. Louis. To lead the party Jefferson had named his private secretary, twenty-nine-year-old Captain Meriwether Lewis of the First Regiment of Infantry, and thirty-three-year-old Lieutenant William Clark of the Corps of Artillerists (brevetted Captain for the journey), a younger brother of the famed George Rogers Clark.

Their exploit is legend: the American epic of a small band against a vast land. The glimmers of individuality are lost in the shadows cast by the men marching across the endless prairies, climbing the cruel mountains, riding canoes down the wild rivers into the setting sun. But it really wasn't all treacle and technicolor. There were the miles of mud and the days of dust, the clench of dysentery, the uncertainty about the Indians, the chill shudder of spring thaws, the unending rains of the coastal winter "enough to grow moss on a musket," the frustration of rivers that curved off in the wrong direction, the burning misery of "the venereals," the disappointment of passes that butted dead ends. These trials the men met with grumbling and complaint and fear, for they were not demigods, though even the exploits among the fascinated tribeswomen of Clark's Negro slave, York, have taken on the aspects of mythology.

Behind the images of the bronze statues striding determinedly westward it is not easy to make out the real and uncertain humans, but they were there. Perhaps someone should erect a statue to commemorate that very human moment when the party was coming back down the Missouri and, near the mouth of the Yellowstone, Peter Crusat mistook Captain Lewis for an elk in the brush and shot him through the buttocks ("a very severe stroke," wrote the recipient), to that hero's continuing discomfort when seated in canoe or St. Louis banquet hall.

The best antidote to the lard of glamour rubbed on by the myth makers is a dose of the captains' Journals, those magnificently misspelled documents with their wonderful, matter-of-fact detail. In the Journals the humans are very human. Here is Patrick Gass, chunky and short, an old soldier full of gripes and competence. Here Peter Crusat, half-blind but an experienced riverman—whose counsel, though erratic, was respected. And here the brutal, lecherous trader, Toussaint Charbonneau, who was hired by the explorers during their winter at Mandan on the Missouri for his knowledge of the land ahead and of the Indians, but whose slave-girl wife, the pregnant squaw whom Charbonneau had won on the gambling blanket, was to prove the most memorable addition to the party.

She was Sacajawea: "the first girl scout" to the romantic, "every man's woman" to those knowledgeable of the fate of female captives among the Minni-tarees. She had been falsely credited with guiding the party across the mountains; she was almost useless as a guide but of great service as a passport (or at least a visa) through much Indian country, since her presence assured some tribes that the corps was not a war party, and her reunion with her own people, the Shoshones, assured their co-operation. The facts in the Journals are more fascinating than myth: Sacajawea in difficult labor, delivering her baby within ten minutes of being administered powdered rattlesnake rattle (though, as the captains cautiously observe, "the effect the rattle may have had might be difficult to determine.") Sacajawea, Charbonneau, Clark, and the baby trapped in a gully by a flash flood ("a roling torrent with irrisistable force driving rocks mud and everything before it"), with the slave York appearing at the last moment to haul them to safety. Sacajawea talking to the hair seals off the Oregon Coast, convinced they were really Indians. Most dramatic of all, Sacajawea starting to translate at a council with the Shoshones and suddenly recognizing in Camaahwait, the chief, her own brother.

Having crossed the Rockies and encountered the Shoshones, the party looked forward to a downhill glide to the ocean, but the going was far from good. The Shoshones gave directions to the Salmon River, which was reputed to lead to "the great stinking lake," as they called the ocean. Clark scouted it but decided the corps could survive neither the Salmon's rapids nor its foodless countryside. So, with an Indian guide whom they called Old Toby, the party turned north. They struggled through the Bitterroots ("Steep & ruged") until, near starvation, they achieved the Lolo Pass and emerged on the westward flowing Clearwater, amid the Nez Percés, who fattened them on dog meat, which all but Clark came to like and even Clark described as "a helthy strong diet."

The Nez Percés still tell of the arrival of the party near Kamiah in Idaho. York paddled one of the captains and Sacajawea across the Clearwater to the village, and the sight of a white man, a black man, and a red woman in the canoe sent the whole village fleeing into the hills.

On the Clearwater, a good canoe stream, the explorers manufactured four large canoes and a small one, in which they swept downriver to the Snake, down the Snake to the Columbia itself. Occasionally a canoe was split on the rocks but they managed to make repairs with "Knees & Strong peces" and keep going. In bad stretches they sometimes lowered the empty dugouts on lines. Clark has described the successful passage of the falls at the head of the Dalles, the eight-mile canyon where the river fights across the backbone of the Cascades:

> As the portage of our canoes over this high rock would be impossible with our Strength, and the only danger in passing thro those narrows was the whorls and swills arriseing from the Compression of the water, and which I thought (as also our principal waterman Peter Crusat) by good Stearing we could pass down Safe, accordingly I determined to pass through this place not with standing the horred appearance of this agitated gut swelling, boiling and whorling in every direction which from the top of the rock did not appear as bad as when I was in it; however we passed Safe to the astonishment of all the Inds of the last Lodges who viewed us from the top of the rock.

Farther down the Dalles they were forced to portage, and the Indians they hired to help them stole them blind, even taking their peace pipe. But after that they were on the open water, with only the weather for antagonist. And soon came the day when the river broadened until it looked like "this great Pacific Octean which we have been so long anxious to See. and the roreing or noise made by the waves breaking on the rocky Shores (as I suppose) may be heard distinctly."

On November 7, 1805, Clark wrote in his notebook: "Ocian in view! O! the joy."

Their joy was diluted by a series of rainstorms that swept in off the Pacific and kept the Corps pinned in soggy discomfort to the narrow beach on the north shore of the river.

Monday, Nov. 11 ... the wind verry high from the S.W. with most tremendious waves breaking with great violence against the Shores, rain falling in torrents, we all wet as usial—and our situation is truly a disagreeable one; the great quantities of rain which has loosened the stones on the hill Sides; and the Small stones fall down upon us, our canoes at one place at the mercy of the waves, our baggage in another; and our selves and party Scattered on floating logs and Such dry spots as can be found on the hill sides, and crivicies of the rocks. ...

Tuesday, Nov. 12—A tremendious thunder storm abt 3 oClock this morning accompanied by wind from the S W. and Hail, this Storm of hard clap's of thunder Lighting and hail untill about 6 o'Clock at intervales It then became light for a short time when the heavens became darkened by a black cloud from the S.W. & a hard rain suckceeded which last until 12 oClock with a hard wind which raised the seas tremendiously high braking with great force and fury against the rocks & trees on which we lie, as our situation became seriously dangerous, we took advantage of a low tide and moved our camp around a point a short distance. ...

Friday, Nov. 15 ... The Sun Shown untill 1 oClock P.M. which afford us time to Dry our bedding and examine the baggage which I found nearly all wet, Some of our pounded fish Spoiled in the wet, I examined the ammunition and caused all the arms to be put in order. about 3 oClock the wind luled, and the river became calm, I had the canoes loaded in great haste and Set Out, from this dismal nitch where we have been confined without the possibility of proceeding on, returning to a better Situation, or get out to hunt; Scerce of Provisions, and torents of rain poreing on us all the time. proceeded on passed the blustering point below which I found a butifull Sand beech thro which runs a Small river from the hills, below the mouth of the Stream is a *village* of 36 houses uninhabited by anything except flees. ... As the tide was comeing in and the Seas became verry high immediately from the *ocian* immediately faceing us I landed and formed a camp on the highest spot I could find between the hight of the tides ... this I could plainly See would be the extent of our journey by water, as the waves were too high at any stage for our Canoes to proceed any further down.

A few days on the exposed north shore convinced Lewis and Clark that it was no place to spend the winter. They crossed the wide river and looked for a more favorable site. Clark paused long enough to carve on a great tree an American reply to the message Mackenzie had painted on the rocks to the north:

William Clark December 3rd 1805. By
land from the U. States in 1804 1805.

After the captains found an area of high ground suitable for winter camp, the men packed their remaining supplies up to it, floundering across "bogs which

The wet winds from the Pacific, rising over the coastal mountains, cool and lose their capacity to hold moisture. They deposit their freight from the ocean as rain or snow upon the western ranges —the Cascades, the Olympics, the Blues, the Coeur d'Alenes, the Selkirks, the Rockies. Through the winter and into spring the moisture is held in snow and ice, to be withdrawn gradually during the hot months of summer and the dry months of early fall.

Below the great snowfields stand the forests, and they, too, slow the run-off from the storms. This is a view of the Cascade Range in Washington, from the crest of Mount St. Helens.

Waterfalls are plentiful in the Columbia River Gorge. At right: Fairy Falls, a mile or so by trail above Benson State Park in Oregon.

In the spring, snows start to recede and pools appear. Here is a mountain lake at the foot of Mount Garibaldi in British Columbia.

OPPOSITE: *The rivers wear deep canyons in the ro Oneonta Gorge east of Portland is one of the most s tacular canyons of streams flowing from the Cascades i the Columbia River Gorge.*

A bend of the Yakima River between Yakima and Ellensburg, Washington.

The Snake River threads its tortuous way through Hell's Canyon between Idaho and Oregon. Hell's Canyon is the deepest canyon in the United States.

A rainstorm moving eastward through the Columbia River Gorge.

44

the wate of a man would shake for ½ an Acre." Working in rain that chilled their bones and rotted their leather clothing, they raised within a month eight cabins, set facing inward across a compound, the rear walls making up part of a stockade. Patrick Gass, the stocky carpenter, exulted in the qualities of the towering western red cedar which made "the streightest and most butifullest logs" and could be "split ten feet long and two broad, not more than an inch and a half thick." The camp was named Fort Clatsop, after the Indians on whose land it stood.

The Clatsops were friendly, too friendly for the well-being of the corps. The tribeswomen, partly from sheer good will and Indian customs of hospitality, partly from avarice, did their level best to make the men comfortable. The leaders, to keep the corpsmen from providing their girl friends with the camp cutlery and other hardware in return for intangibles, "divided some ribin between the men of our party to bestow on their favourite Lasses." In return the girls presented the men with the social diseases that the earlier sea traders had left with the tribe.

Female companionship was the only thing the men had in abundance. They ran out of salt and tobacco. Food was so short that even Clark came to speak admiringly of dog stew; Lewis found it "very far superior to the horse in any state." In vain they watched for a trading ship or the government supply vessel that Jefferson inexplicably failed to dispatch. When the time came for the return journey, supplies were so low that Lewis gave up his gold-laced dress-uniform coat as part payment on a dugout suitable for upstream navigation. "I think," he noted, "the U' States are indebted to me another Uniform coat for that of which I have disposed on this occasion was but little woarn."

On September 23, 1806, the corps swept downstream into St. Louis, dispelling the rumors that they had been killed by Indians or captured by Spaniards and set to work mining silver in Mexico. They were so delighted to be approaching civilization that a herd of cows grazing on the banks of the Missouri was "a joyfull Sight to our party and caused a Shout to be raised for joy." The party itself was a joyful sight to the citizens of St. Louis, the journals noting that "the people gathred on the Shore and Hizzared three cheers."

There was much for the merchants of St. Louis to cheer. The captains and the corps had proved that the Rockies could be crossed and that the Columbia was indeed a highway to the Pacific. The door to the intermountain storehouse of furs had been forced; what remained was for men with the right combination of imagination and toughness to exploit the opportunity. Adventurers were not lacking.

There was the Spaniard, Manuel Lisa, who, along with Clark and ten others, set up the Missouri Fur Company and pushed the trading area deep into the mountains, claiming with considerable justice, "I appear as a benefactor, not a pillager of the Indian. My blacksmiths work incessantly for them, charging nothing. I lend them traps, only demanding a preference in their trade. My establishments are the refuge of the weak and of the old men no longer able to follow their lodges. . . ." With Lisa pointing the way to profits by trading with the Indians for the Indians' good, other Americans were sure to follow.

To the north the partners of the North West Company continued their attempts to link the beaver streams and the otter shores into a single fur empire. There was the dour Simon Fraser, more durable than thoughtful, grappling with the stubborn geology of the Fraser Basin. And there was David Thompson, the self-taught astronomer, who became the first man to follow the full course of the Columbia.

The Indians who watched Thompson studying the heavens through his brass sextant called him Koo-koo-sint, the Man Who Watches Stars. They told him they were sure that when he scanned the skies "The Great Spirit speaks to you, and tells you of what we know nothing." Thompson tried to tell the Indians what he knew; contemporary journals often picture him seated on a log by a campfire, translating the Bible for his companions. Unlike most fur traders, Thompson eschewed alcohol for either personal use or trade. Once when ordered by superiors to take rum across the mountains, he confessed to his journal, "I placed the kegs on a vicious horse, and by noon the Kegs were empty and in pieces . . . I wrote my partners what I had done, and that I would do the same for every Keg of Alcohol."

Thompson it was who, carrying his Bible and accompanied by his Chippewa wife, descended the little Blaeberry from the Rockies to its meeting with a great river, a stream a thousand yards wide that charged out of the southeast and rolled northward along the shoulder of another mountain range. Thompson traced the stream back to its headwaters. Eventually convinced that this was the Columbia, he returned another year and, after numerous delays, "set off on a voyage down the Columbia River to explore this river in order to open out a passage for the interior trade with the Pacific Ocean."

At the confluence of the Snake and the Columbia he landed to post a half sheet of paper:

> Knowing hereby that this country is claimed by Great Britain as part of its territorieis and that the N. W. Company of Merchants from Canada . . . do hereby intend to erect a factory in this place for the commerce of the country around. D. Thompson. Junction of the Sawpatin River with the Columbia. July 9, 1811.

On July 15, 1811, Thompson came into view of the Pacific "which to me was a great pleasure, but my Men seemed disappointed; they had been accustomed to the boundless horizon of the great Lakes of Canada, and their high rolling waves; from the Ocean they expected a more boundless view, a something beyond the power of their senses, which they could not describe."

There was disappointment for Thompson, too. On the south shore of the river he could make out a clearing. Investigation proved it to be "the fur trading post of Mr. J. J. Astor of the City of New York; which was four low log huts . . . The place was in charge of Messrs. McDougall and Stuart who had been clerks of the North West Company; and by whom we were politely received."

No business venture in Northwest history was to prove more ill-starred than John Jacob Astor's Pacific Fur Company. Two parties were sent west, one by land from St. Louis, the other by sea. The waterborne expedition had reached the Columbia on April 11 after a fearsome voyage around Cape Horn and a desperate crossing of the Columbia Bar in which eight men, ordered out in small boats to probe for the channel, were drowned. After the party hurriedly selected a poor site for the trading post of Astoria, the *Tonquin* sailed north on a trading mission but was captured by the Indians at Clayoquot Sound, all the officers and all but one crewman perishing.

The overland party, after an appalling series of misadventures, recklessly tried to run the white waters of the Snake, losing five of their fifteen canoes before abandoning the attempt and setting out cross-country in midwinter. Some gave up and wintered with the Indians, some disappeared, and those who reached Astoria were too bedraggled and dispirited to add much strength to the beleaguered post.

The outbreak of the War of 1812 had left Astoria exposed to seizure by either the North West Company forces or the British Navy, which was reported to have dispatched ships from London to clear the Pacific Coast of Americans. Desperately the influential fur merchant John Jacob Astor (who was in the process of loaning the government some two million dollars to prosecute the war) urged the State Department to see that his trading post was protected. "Even yet it is not too Late to Do good if our government would act with promptness," he wrote. "I have not time to point out all the advantages that would result from Securing the River to us." The government promised to dispatch a frigate, but did not send it. A supply ship Astor had sent earlier, the *Lark,* was wrecked in the Hawaiian Islands. A ship chartered by the Astorians on the coast refused to return with supplies when its captain learned of the war. The men on the river felt deserted.

The only bright spot was that trading had gone well. A company clerk, Alexander Ross, in a trading shack at the juncture of the Columbia and the Okanogan (spelled Okanagan in Canada) found that he could get a beaver skin in return for five tobacco leaves, twenty prime skins for a yard of white cotton.

During his first season, Ross estimated that in return for items worth $175 in Boston he received 1550 beaver skins worth $11,250 on the Canton market.

Other areas proved less lucrative. Trapping in the country south of the Columbia and along the Snake was more dangerous than rewarding. So when in the fall of 1813 no supply ships had come but, instead, a party of seventy-five tough and well-armed North West Company *voyageurs* descended the Columbia and pitched camp on the flats below the outpost, the Astorians decided it would be prudent to sell out. They relinquished 17,000 pounds of baled beaver fur and 2000 miscellaneous skins for $40,000, while the North West Company agreed to pay a ten-per-cent mark-up above cost for the trading goods still on hand in the fort, and to hire at prevailing salaries such workers as wished to switch allegiance.

The deal was consummated on October 16, 1813. Six weeks later, H. M. S. *Raccoon,* twenty-six guns, showed up off Astoria. Her captain was chagrined that the transfer had been arranged on a commercial basis rather than at gunpoint, and could not forego the pleasure of staging a military ceremony at which he ran up the British flag over the former American post. "Country and fort I have taken possession of in name and for British majesty," he wrote to his superiors on December 5. "Enemies party quite broke up that they have no settlement whatever on this River or Coast." The seizure was to prove not only redundant but an ill-advised diplomatic luxury. John Quincy Adams, who succeeded James Monroe as Secretary of State in 1817, was able to convince the British that the transfer of the fort under the circumstances was an act of war rather than a commercial transaction, and that the Treaty of Ghent called for the return of captured territory. Control of the fort was given back to the United States.

After the purchase, however, the North West Company enjoyed a monopoly of the fur trade west of the mountains. As monopolists they tended to relax, particularly the men at Fort George, as the British had renamed Astoria. Relaxation in earnest began with the arrival of the North West Company supply ship *Isaac Todd* in the spring of 1814. The *Isaac Todd* brought elderly Donald McTavish as governor of the fort, and Governor McTavish brought a protégé, one Jane Barnes, the first white woman on the Columbia.

Jane, who had been a barmaid before embarking on a new career, proved a great social success on the river, with both red men and white coveting her companionship. The son of the Clatsop chief, Concomly, arrived one day to offer a bridal payment of a hundred otter skins (worth perhaps $10,000) and a guarantee that as his bride she would not have to dig camas bulbs or clams, or gather bark, or perform other menial tasks, that she would be premiere among his wives and would retain the right to wear English clothes and smoke as many pipes a day as she wished. Jane saw fit to reject this regal offer, but she did accept an invitation from Alexander Henry to share her bed with him. Henry was another partner in the Company, and considerably younger than the outraged McTavish, who was temporarily reduced to sleeping on a table. Eventually McTavish found an Indian woman to his liking (she bore the odd name of Mrs. Clapp) and he set about furnishing her with a wardrobe to rival Jane's. This high-style competition ended abruptly when McTavish and Henry tried to cross the bar in a small boat and were drowned. Jane packed her finery and caught the next available supply vessel back to England.

While the North West Company partners were relaxed in their arrangements for female companionship at the fort, they set store on punctilio in other phases of social life. Meals were so formal that three pots of tea and three bowls of sugar appeared on the tables, a different grade of leaf and grind of cane for men of different station. Feeling that they deserved both homage and comfort in recompense for their isolation, the executives imported luxuries strange to the wilderness, ostrich plumes and coats of mail for ceremonial wear, fustian and velvet, gloves and umbrellas. Nor did their catering to a craving for the familiar end with dress: to the Northwest Coast, home of the cedar dugout, they ordered from Eastern Canada, by way of London and the Horn, shipments of birch rinds for making birch-bark canoes.

Importing such exotic coals to the Columbian Newcastle for their own use was hardly a source of profit, and the river post showed as a red blotch on the company books. Other factors contributed to the deficit. The Indians along the Snake and south of the Columbia were reluctant to ensnarl themselves in a trap-and-trade economy. The East India Company's insistence on its monopoly rights in China made it difficult for the North West Company to sell its fur in the most profitable market. The Nor'westers' great rival, the Hudson's Bay Company, had come under the control of the imaginative Lord Selkirk, who undertook to set up colonies of Scottish farmers along the Red River, an undertaking which added to the competition between the companies the burden of the traditional hatred of the hunter for the man who brings the wilderness under cultivation. Civil war broke out between the companies, a war of ambush, of hijacking or sabotage, and of occasional pitched battles. Actual fighting did not extend to the North West Company's preserve on the Columbia, but the struggle distracted the attention and drained the energy of the leaders. Since the most trusted *voyageurs* were needed for active duty on the other side of the Rockies, the Nor'westers found it necessary to import contingents of eastern Indians, mainly Iroquois and Abenaki, to make up the fur brigades on the Columbia, and these exotic strangers often became embroiled in little wars of their own with the local tribes. To this day the Cowlitz hate the Iroquois.

Still, not all was chaos in the Columbia Division. Along the middle reaches of the Columbia and the Snake (far from the fleshpots of Fort George) the tributaries were traced, horse trails between the river systems were established, and in the areas where the Indians refused to devote themselves to the trapline company employees worked the streams.

A lonely business, beaver trapping. The fur brigades would assemble at the inland forts in the spring and after a ceremonious regale, or drunk, move back into the mountains. A brigade would consist of thirty or forty men, mostly Indians, with canoes or horses or both for transport. Back in beaver country the brigades would divide into parties of six or eight, and these in turn would separate each day into units of two or three men who would work along the branches of a stream, looking for the meadows or meanders where the water was slow enough to be dammed. In such stretches, often enough, beavers had dropped trees across the stream as the bulwark for a dam, and at the end of the pool formed by the obstruction built a house of small branches plastered with half a foot of mud.

If they could find the slide where the beaver entered the pool from the bank, the trappers set their five-pound traps below water and anchored them by a steel chain fastened to a stake. But if the slide could not be found, they put traps where there were signs of beaver and baited them with wands dipped in musk from the preputial glands of beaver, a noisome secretion the trappers carried in plugged horn bottles, the use of which rendered beaver trappers distinguishable from other mortals in the dark and at a distance.

Traps were usually set between sunset and dark, the men wading considerable distances up the stream to put them in place and returning to raise them at dawn. The beavers were usually skinned on the spot, the scent glands removed, and, if the distance to camp was not too far, the tail carried back for food. (The tough outer skin was burned off, the inner flesh boiled.) The daylight hours were spent in camp scraping the pelts and stretching them on willow frames, or scouting the streams for new trap locations. Camps were shifted every day or two. The brigades might be gone as long as six months, and few returned without having lost at least one member to accident, Indians, or desertion.

The destinies of scantly populated areas are controlled by decisions made elsewhere, the Northwest proving no exception. The diplomats negotiating the end of the War of 1812 had stipulated that the Pacific Fur Company's buildings were to be considered American property (though Britain maintained her over-all claim to the entire Oregon country); John Jacob Astor in New York was no longer interested in Astoria, so the North West Company continued to use the old buildings at Fort George. And then Lord Selkirk of Hudson's Bay Company and Alexander Mackenzie of the North West Company, those inflexible men, died. In 1821 their survivors decided to end the war of the beaver kingdom and consolidate under the convenient charter of the older company. Thus Hudson's Bay Company came to the Pacific Northwest.

George Simpson, the tough little Scot chosen by the Hudson's Bay Company to administer its affairs in America, was told to determine whether the Columbia Division should be abandoned. Governor Simpson took with him on an inspection trip the hulking, prematurely gray, forty-year-old Dr. John McLoughlin, an ex-Nor'Wester, his senior in both years and experience. They met on Athabaska pass, and Simpson preserved his impression of his subordinate in a report to London:

> He was such a figure as I would not like to meet in a dark night in one of the bye lanes in the neighborhood of London, dressed in Clothes that had once been fashionable, but now covered with a thousand patches of different Colors, his beard would do honor to the chin of a Grizzly Bear, his face and hands evidently Shewing that he had not lost much time at his Toilette, loaded with Arms and with his own hurculean dimensions forming a tout ensamble that would convey a good idea of the high way men of former Days.

The impeccable Simpson and the shaggy McLoughlin swept down the Columbia on this inspection trip, liking little of what they found at the posts. "Everything on the Columbia, except the Trade, is on too extended a scale," Simpson declared. He compared the traders' predilection for European provisions to a taste for eating gold, and suggested that salmon become the mainstay of their diet. ("The River, with a potatoe garden, will abundantly maintain a Post.") But the more they saw of the Columbia country, the more they were convinced that it could be useful to the Company—if nothing else, as a buffer against the encroachments of American trappers who were beginning to spill over the barrier of the Rockies, carrying free trade into the area reserved by royal charter for the monopoly.

Britain and America had agreed to joint occupancy of the territory until a boundary could be agreed upon. Since the Columbia then seemed a probable dividing line, Governor Simpson decided that Fort George on the south shore should be abandoned and a new post built on the north side. McLoughlin, assigned to choose a site, selected one a hundred and fifteen miles upstream from the bar and six miles above the point where the Willamette joins the Columbia. Simpson approved. Land was cleared, shelters were erected, and at sunrise on Saturday, March 19, 1825, the "Gentlemen, Servants, Chiefs & Indians" were ordered out to watch Simpson dedicate the new headquarters. "I Baptised it by breaking a Bottle of Rum on the Flag Staff and repeating the following words in a loud voice, 'In behalf of the Honble Hudson's Bay Co^y I hereby name this Establishment Fort Vancouver God Save King George the 4th' with three cheers." Simpson ordered drinks for all, Indians included.

Under the new dispensation the Columbia Division was remade, from a semi-military satrapy, supplied from across the world and extracting a tribute in furs from the territory it occupied, into a nearly self-sustaining organization that ran the wilderness under its control as a fur farm while growing on the lands around its trading posts more than enough cereal, beef, and mutton for company use.

The quest for furs was pressed, new posts were opened, the take in pelts from areas the company expected to keep was regulated, while the territory expected to fall into the hands of the Americans was largely trapped out. To offset the competition of the Yankee sea peddlers in the coves and inlets of the coast, Fort Langley was built at the mouth of the Fraser and smaller outposts opened farther north; later the posts were closed and trade carried on by the steamer *Beaver*, first of her kind on the coast. The *Beaver* burned a fantastic thirty to forty cords of wood a day, and Dr. John McLaughlin came to look on her as an extravagant novelty, but she helped impress the Indians with the Company's omnipotence. "She can do everything except talk," the Indians said. The Yankee sea captains might undercut Hudson's Bay prices on trading goods but they had no attraction to match the ship that moved without sails or paddles.

In a further attempt to wipe out the free-lance competition of the Yankee captains, Hudson's Bay Company entered into an agreement with the Russian-American Company settling jurisdictional disputes along the northern coast line and arranging for the Hudson's Bay Company to supply the Russian settlements in Alaska with foodstuffs.

To raise this extra food, McLoughlin planted retired *voyageurs* on farms along the Cowlitz River and on the Nisqually plain of southern Puget Sound, eventually organizing a subsidiary called the Puget's Sound Agricultural Company. "The Mutton Company," disgusted old-timers called it, and behind their derision lay the age-old fear of the hunter for the encroaching farmer. "Do not . . . my friend suppose that I am myself Smitten with this colonization mania of ours," wrote one old Hudson's Bay fur trader. "That a large population may in course of time Spring up over this country I do not at all doubt, but with one eye one can see the motley crew of which it must necessarily be composed: it will be of every cast and hue into which the naturalist has subdivided the three primary branches that first peopled mother earth."

And indeed it was the possibility of free land—land suitable for farming—that drew the Americans across the mountains in such numbers that by 1846 they had rendered most of the Columbia River valley unprofitable for the Great Company of Gentlemen Adventurers' Trading into Hudson's Bay, and England agreed to the give up claims to the land below the 49th parallel while the United States abandoned its demand for everything up to 54-40.

The RIVERS

...... *now*

The Columbia, great turbulent river of the West, rises quietly enough from a flat stretch of glacial silt 2619 feet above sea level in a valley in eastern British Columbia. Two hundred yards to the west the first foothills of the Selkirks—logged, burned, and jagged with blackened stumps—hide the bare granite peaks; to the east a stark plain lifts slowly toward the Rockies. Across the mountains some eighty miles to the northeast is Banff; the same distance to the southwest, Idaho and Montana meet British Columbia. The clear water appears silent and unbubbled and flows north along the valley.

Columbia Lake, which receives the young river only a mile from its source at Canal Flats, is thirteen miles long, two and a half miles wide. The stream, barely twenty feet across when it enters the lake, emerges as a major river, though placid, an easy river for boatmen until it passes through the lovely Windermere Lakes. Then the mountains press in on the river. The Rockies hulk high to the east, a barrier of glittering rock and snow with patches of forest imposed darkly on the lower slopes. The river has widened to two hundred feet but under the looming mountains seems smaller; peak after peak thrusts above the ten-thousand-foot level; the connecting ridge—the sharp-edged backbone of the continent—stands so high that any dip below a mile forms an important pass. Here the Columbia gathers strength from the meltflow of the greatest icefields south of the Arctic. Beyond the Windermeres the river is always powerful and often dangerous. Surprise Rapids and Death Rapids lie ahead.

For nearly a sixth of its 1270 miles, the river slants off to the northwest along the shoulder of the Selkirks. Then another range, the Cariboos, blocks its path and, dramatically, the river turns to the southwest, toward the fertile lands of the Palouse, the timbered Cascades, toward the accessible Pacific. Although a recently negotiated international agreement provides for Canadian-American construction of dams in the Canadian Big Bend, this stretch remains unbroken, almost unchanged, the river an unchained force shouldering aside tremendous mountains.

As it nears the Washington border, the river slows and swells into the 150-mile lagoon held in by the Grand Coulee dam. As it crosses the boundary into the United States, it is now 500 miles long, but is only a hundred miles west of its source at Canal Flats. Just before leaving Canada it absorbs the waters of an American-born tributary, Clark Fork (the Pend Oreille), which drains out of Lake Pend Oreille in Idaho and discharges into the Columbia as much water as the Colorado gives the sea.

Held in by the mighty masonry downstream, the Columbia flows gently south, a man-made lake lapping over former rapids and waterfalls. A hundred miles south of Canada it adds the lovely Spokane to its conquests, then turns west to run over and through the prison of Grand Coulee Dam, only to find itself entrapped again by Chief Joseph, that jewel among Columbia dams.

Below Joseph the river is momentarily free and speeds austerely through broad valleys of basalt to its rendezvous with the Okanogan, which supplies a last invigorating infusion of Canadian water. Southward the Columbia is ponded and employed by a series of dams—Wanapum, Priest Rapids, Rock Island. It moves through apple and apricot orchards around Wenatchee, the irrigated wheatlands, and the bleak sunburnt wastes of the Atomic Energy Commission preserves above Hanford, then curves briefly eastward to meet the Snake.

To the Columbia, the Snake brings the waters of a stream three times longer than the Hudson and more powerful. The joined streams swing west to avoid the Blue Mountains of Oregon, once the western promontory of the continent. Until recently the Columbia butted through the Cascades over a series of fearsome rapids; now it rests ponded behind McNary, John Day, and Bonneville Dams, its giant strength under man's restraint.

Below Bonneville the Columbia combats the tidal pulse as it sweeps, imperious as an ocean, to its rendezvous with the Pacific. The great river turns majestically north after passing Portland, then bends back westward for the last time and sweeps down the broadening estuary until it hurls itself across the chaos of sand and foam, "the bare ribs of the continent, that seven-shoaled horror, the Columbia Bar," and disappears.

The Army Engineers have remade the channel through the bar, and ships now pass in relative safety through waters that have claimed more vessels than any other passage in the world. The ships move upstream almost as safely as the salmon and almost as far.

The return of the salmon is one of the most beautiful facts of life in the Pacific Northwest. Five different species of salmon come to life in the gravel beds of our streams. The young fish find their way downstream to salt water, disappear for years (some have been caught as far away as Siberia) and then, answering a mysterious call, find their way back across the ocean to their native river. They fight back upstream, through rapids and over falls, often back to the very tributary where they were born; and over the gravel beds from which they emerged, the females hover while they drop their eggs, the males unloose clouds of sperm, the sand and gravel stirred by the beat of their powerful tails swirls protectingly over the fertilized eggs; life begins and the parent salmon swim away and die.

The life cycle of the Pacific salmon remains nearly as much a mystery to twentieth-century scientists as it was to the Indians. Researchers theorize that the salmon find their way back across the ocean by using the sun as compass, somehow adjusting to the time of day; they theorize that once in fresh water, the salmon use remembered shapes, an instinct for upstream movement, and an extraordinarily delicate sense of smell to nose out their home stream. But the theories raise as many questions as they answer.

The Indians, with their anthropomorphic conviction that all living things were human beings in another form, believed that the salmon returned simply to bring food to the tribe. The first fish taken from the annual run was greeted ceremoniously as a welcome guest and relative. Lewis and Clark, on their trip back up the Columbia in 1806, happened to be at the Dalles when the Indians received the first representative of the spring run. "The whole village," the Journals note with marvel, "was filled with rejoicing at having caught a single salmon."

Among the tribesmen at the Dalles the man who caught the first fish was required to lay it carefully on the bank, head upstream, so that salmon who were following would continue to swim upstream. The fishermen then called the other men of the village. When all were assembled he picked up the pioneer fish and carried it to his house. A medicine man delivered a speech of greeting to the salmon, then cut off its flanks, leaving the head, backbone, and tail in one piece; he made incisions at short intervals in each of the flanks and inserted bits of dry cedar to hold the cuts open. The backbone piece was cleaned with fern leaves, never with water. Stones arranged to form a flat surface were heated by a wood fire in a shallow pit. When the wood was consumed, a thick layer of chokeberry leaves was heaped over the hot stones, pieces of salmon were placed on the leaves, and mats were put over the salmon. When the fish was roasted, the whole village assembled in communion and each received a small piece to eat.

Salmon deserved a ceremonious welcome. Historians estimate that the fifty thousand Indians along the Northwest rivers caught each year eighteen million pounds of salmon. The white man's welcome has been less friedly to the salmon. Dams now block an estimated sixty percent of the spawning beds, and despite the great increase in the efficiency of commercial fishing equipment, and the swarming numbers of sports fishermen, the total catch now is estimated to be three million pounds a year less than the Indian take in the old days. The extent to which this is attributable to dams and pollution rather than to over-fishing and climatic changes is obscure. But between fishermen and dam builders rages one of the most important political-economic struggles of the area. Fortunately there are growing indications that ways will be found to keep the lovely, protein-packed salmon coursing back from the sea while permitting still more dams to turn the power of the river into energy for the cities and farms and factories of the Northwest Corner.

Salmon jumping from pool to pool on their way over Oregon City Falls of the Willamette River as they journey hundreds of miles from the Pacific to spawn in some remote mountain stream.

57

Salmon fishing off Point Roberts, Washington.

Fishing is one of the most cosmopolitan activities. Men from many nations man the fishing fleet. During the winter months when the fleet is in and the fishermen are mending their nets, you can see at any wharf where the boats tie up, faces from faraway places.

North Sea

Baltic

Mediterranean

ALL PHOTOS BY JOSEF SCAYLEA

Scandinavia

Dalmatian Coast

*And an American Indian, whose ances-
tors met the others when they came.*

The FORESTS
......then

TREES ARE plants. To most pioneers, they were weeds. The great stands of Douglas fir and hemlock and western cedar—"Thick as the hair on a dog's back, reaching to God's elbow, so tall it takes two men and a boy to see to the top of one tree"—were considered liabilities to the land, prehistoric leftovers, as inconvenient as a herd of dinosaurs. Most settlers avoided the forest and sought the natural clearings.

The forest was conceded to have some uses. From the first, ships' captains admired the tall, slim trees that stood close to shoreline, branchless for as much as a hundred feet: ideal masts. John Meares cut a deckload of spars on Vancouver Island in 1788, though he had to jettison them while fighting a storm in mid-Pacific. George Vancouver replaced a spar on the *Discovery* while charting Puget Sound. John Jacob Astor dreamed of milling lumber for export to the Russians in Alaska, and one of the men left over from the Astor expedition built for the Hudson's Bay Company the first sawmill in the northwest, a water-driven mill at La Camas, six miles above Fort Vancouver; in 1827 it was cutting 3000 feet a day. The first Americans to settle on Puget Sound earned some of their supplies by cutting wooden bolts for the British at Fort Nisqually, and the pioneers at Seattle found a cash crop in piling needed for docks built in San Francisco. In 1855 a load of prime spars was sent to the French Naval Yard at Brest and attracted so much attention that the British Navy placed an order for a similar shipment in 1857. But the crucial development was the introduction of steam as the driving power for the saws.

In 1853 Henry Yesler, a stocky, bearded lumberman from Ohio, opened a steam sawmill at Seattle. By the time the Civil War started, thirty-one more mills were eating into the forests. In 1870 the cut in Washington Territory—the leading producer—was 130 million board feet, and lumbering accounted for all but five per cent of the industrial employment of the region.

A new style of logging developed. The sawmills squatted at tidewater, their wharfs thrust out into the harbor, their skid roads reaching back into the forests. The skid road was made of logs, from a foot to a foot-and-a-half in diameter, laid crosswise to the road. These logs were peeled and usually notched to guide the logs pulled from the forest by teams of oxen, called bulls, or sometimes by mules or horses, down the skid road to the mill. A greaser, or grease monkey, usually Indian, ran ahead of the ox teams swabbing the notches in the skid-road logs to ease the passage of the load. "A greaser does not need much brains," a contemporary observer noted, "but he desperately wants a reliable stomach. The grease used was mostly dogfish liver, which had a smell to be noticed not only nearby but at a distance. A blind man could follow a skid road recently greased, if he had a nose, or half a nose."

The skid roads led to the mills, and since the towns grew up around the mills the skid roads became the pathways to the towns. Along the roads, businessmen set their traps for visitors: bars, and hotels, and hotels with bars and girls. These increased the attraction of the towns to the men back in the woods, and stimulated the frequency with which the men who worked in the woods found their way to town. At one end of the skid roads lay work; at the other, pleasure. The logs on the skid roads were set at even distances, and the loggers walking to and fro along the roads developed a shuffle and hop distinctive to their time and place. The sailors they met in the milltown joints chided the loggers for their "skid-road gait."

Power-driven saws could slice logs faster than nature could grow new trees. When it was no longer practical to haul the logs overland to the mills, skid roads reached in from the clay banks. Logs were dragged to the water and herded into corrals made of long boomsticks linked by chains. Towboats of limited power but colorful history (one had been a Russian gunboat which came under United States colors with the purchase of Alaska) pulled the rafts to the millponds to await sawing. To say a lumberman had "logs in the pond" was to praise his financial standing.

The boards of Puget Sound, like the wheat of the Inland Empire, were loadstones that attracted the ships of the world. The ships clustered, three and four deep, at the docks to take their turns loading the sweet-smelling cedar, the sharp-scented fir, or an occasional load of sour hemlock, though hemlock was widely scorned as a weed tree and captains preferred not to load it since its greater density made the ships ride deep and travel slow. No Plimsoll lines regulated cargo in that era; ships frequently were towed to the strait with their decks almost awash. If a captain protested overloading, he would be innocently asked, "But how can you sink a ship loaded with lumber?" The standard reply was, "I don't know how you can sink her and I don't know how you can steer her."

Since lumber is not perishable, the lumber trade became the recourse for the sailing ships whose glory was being dimmed by steam. A cliché of the 1880s on Puget Sound was "the forest of spars growing at dockside." They were there, all right; the great ships of another day. But the square-sailed vessels of the white-winged fleet—the ship, the bark, the barkentine—were not meant for the lumber trade. Their hatches, designed for cargoes of spices and teas and silks, were inadequate for engorging long boards; it was necessary to cut in new ports on the bow and stern of the old square-riggers, well above the water line. The full-rigged vessels required larger and more experienced crews than did craft with fore and aft sails on the aftermasts. They were big and beautiful, but like an ancient automobile they were not designed for latter-day traffic.

Once the marine underwriters' association office in San Francisco decided that Douglas fir, suitably seasoned and salted, was as good for shipbuilding as oak, if not better (it gripped nails more firmly, and iron set in Douglas fir did not corrode as quickly as that set in oak), a Puget Sound shipbuilding industry developed. Northwest yards in the 1880s sent onto the oceans a new type of vessel, the lumber schooner. Smaller but just as capacious as the older craft, it had easily accessible holds, much clear deck space, and fore-and-aft sails on all three masts; it required fewer crewmen—which is to say that it gave better mileage. The schooner concept was pushed until there came into being in 1891 the five-masted, bald-headed schooner, which had no topsails and could run with only two men to a watch—one for the lookout, one at the wheel.

Meanwhile, logging was changing. The near-to-coast areas were logged out. Trees had to be found farther and farther from the mills and from the water. An enterprising logger gave up on dragging the logs directly to mill or water, and hit on the device of running wooden rails back into the forest and hauling carloads of logs to the saws or tidewater. At first these carloads were moved by horsepower in the form of real horses, but before long somebody—the Blackman brothers at Marysville, most authorities agree—imported a little steam locomotive, a dinky. Now the way was open for lumbermen to pursue the receding treeline back from water's edge into the foothills and up the sides of the mountains.

With steam power being applied to logging trains, the next step was to use steam instead of oxen to drag the felled trees to trackside for loading. The concept of a donkey engine occurred almost simultaneously to several men working in the woods, but John Dolbeer won the race to the Patent Office. Dolbeer's donkey was an upright steam engine with a single vertical cylinder that turned a winch, thereby winding a line around a drum and inching the attached log toward the yarding area. Weak and cranky though the early donkeys were, they drove the living horses and bulls from the forests. In charge of the contraptions were engineers known as donkey punchers; they waited beside the engine while choker-men wrestled a heavy wire noose into place around a log, and the hook tender— a man whose occupation called for the extraordinary combination of the strength of a wrestler and the touch of a surgeon—attached the cable to the choker. A signalman, called the whistle punk, blew a whistle that told the donkey-puncher it was time to reel in. The machine age had come to the deep forest.

In the mills, too, changes were being made. The old up-and-down blades were replaced by circular saws, six or more feet across, with thirty curved teeth; power carriages were introduced to push the logs into the bite of steel. The mills' capacity to take in timber and spew out lumber grew ever greater.

Nationally, steam power became an enormously powerful political force. When the federal government decided that a prime necessity was transcontinental railroads, it encouraged promoters to build them by offering them vast areas of public domain along the rights of way; these grants could be used to secure capital. It was inevitable that the land grants, considered a noble incentive to progress when offered, would upon the completion of the railroads be regarded in a different light, especially by farmers called upon to pay high freight rates. Farm politicians yelped demands that Congress declare the land grants forfeit, but the railroads— adept at lobbying—emerged from two decades of bitter controversy with their grants intact.

Jim Hill, shaggy and sharply focused, proved to be without peer as a manipulator. The Great Northern had come into possession of titles to land awarded a defunct Dakota line; by threatening to dispossess settlers who had taken up railroad land under the impression it was in the public domain, Hill put the government in a position where it had to offer to trade him sixty-five thousand

The first sawmill in the Northwest was built in the 1820s by the Hudson's Bay Company at La Camas.

Oxen brought the trunks of the forest giants from the woods to the mills. Running ahead of the slow-moving log is the grease monkey, bucket in hand. He greased the skid-logs with dogfish oil so that they would move more easily. The oxen were breveted "bulls" in logging-camp terminology. A good bull driver might be paid more than the governor of the Territory, which was not considerable.

65

The square-rigged Barmbeck *enters the lonely Strait of Juan de Fuca en route to Puget Sound for a cargo of lumber.*

The lumber trade developed its special lumber schooner, with wide hatches for easy loading, a clear deck for deck-loads, and convenient fore and aft sails which required few crewmen to handle. This is the Albert, *outward bound with a deck load twelve feet high.*

"A forest of spars grows at dockside," the editorialists of the 1880s liked to say. *The great square-rigged sailing vessels were diverted to the Puget Sound trade when steamers controlled the more perishable cargoes. These vessels are awaiting cargo at the Skinner and Eddy mill dock at Port Blakely, Washington, on Puget Sound which at that time was said to be the largest mill in the world. It employed 1200 men and daily cut 400,000 board feet of lumber.*

Some of the cooks in lumber camps, the loggers said, had trouble keeping water from burning. A boss cook needed a skin thicker than bark and tougher than ax handles to withstand the rasp of remarks about his talents. But the pride of the handle-bar-mustached cook and his two bull cooks (helpers) in their cookhouse is apparent in this early picture from the Weyerhaeuser files.

Bunkhouse in a logging camp. "Pipe smoke of a stinging smell circled over the bowed heads of loggers, who were tired out from their eleven hours in the wet cold. . . . From the rafters, beams and lines hung wet mackinaws, parrafin pants and underclothes which had been boiled to kill the latest crop of lice. The windows were shut tight and the steam from the drying clothes mixed its powerful various smells with that of bitter-root tobacco burning in caked pipes."—From Big Jim Turner, *by Jim Stevens.*

acres of federal land of his own choosing in return for not driving the Dakota farmers from their soil. He chose carefully cruised timberlands in the Pacific Northwest.

At first, lumbermen helped themselves to timber off government property without bothering to pay. When the Timber and Stone Act of 1878 made it possible for "any citizen or person who has made a declaration of intention of becoming a citizen" to buy 160 acres of timber land at $2.50 an acre, mill owners lined up platoons of sailors and working stiffs and marched them into land offices with claims for convenient forest lands. In reaction, Congress set up the Forest Reserves in 1891, which later became the National Forests. These reserves encompassed considerable property belonging to the railroads, so Congress in 1897 passed the Forest Lieu Act, under which holders of acreage within the reserves could exchange land for government property outside. Jim Hill was more than ready to go along with the government. He swapped an assortment of glaciers and canyons and basalt ridges for a new empire of pine and fir and cedar.

Around the turn of the century, Hill sold 900,000 acres of the land he had accumulated to the Weyerhaeuser Timber Company of St. Paul for six dollars an acre and slashed freight rates to the Midwest to encourage lumber shipments. This opened the way to major lumbering operations not only along the Sound but in the pine forests of eastern Washington, eastern Oregon, and Idaho. Lumber, rather than grain or coal or fish, became economic king of the Northwest.

Originally logging camps and mills suffered from lack of manpower. The lumber historian Ralph Andrews recalls that when Oregon's first steam sawmill was built in Portland not enough men could be rounded up to raise the sixteen-inch-square timbers for the frame. Help was asked of Oregon City but no men could be induced to come. Finally convicts were drafted from the Oregon State Penitentiary. When the mills still had woods nearby, loggers followed the skid roads to and from work. But as logging operations became bigger and the operators chased the trees farther back into the mountains, it was no longer possible for loggers to live in town. Camps were set up back in the woods, and the men came to town only for holidays. The loggers were mainly migrant workers, relicts of society, a class apart—the timber beasts. Most possessed nothing but their work clothes, perhaps a Sunday suit wrapped in a lousy bedroll, and the skills they had acquired while surviving the dangerous tasks of the logging shows, where speed was increasingly equated with profit, and highballing was the command for hurrying up. Some camps were better than others, some bosses understanding—there is a touching letter still in existence in which Sol Simpson, an early camp boss, argued with his superiors for permission to let married men have separate quarters in tents—but in general it was not a time for enlightened paternalism. Self-interest seemed best gauged by the short-term operating cost. The usual attitude toward amenities in camp was, "If you don't like it, mister, get out; it's a free country." Operators spoke of working on the three-crew system: one coming, one working, one going.

The timber beasts moved often, from camp to camp, or from camp back to town. Along the old skid roads—Vancouver's Cordova Street, Seattle's Yesler Way, Portland's Burnside—in the places where loggers were accustomed to come for recreation or recuperation, between the bars and honkytonks and flophouses and pawnshops, stood the slave shops, with their inevitable blackboards:

Ten laborers, free fare, east of mountains, government work, 8 hours, $2.00

Two fallers, $3.75

Donkey engineer, $4.00

Swampers—Riggers—Hard-rock men.

Tie makers. Idaho. 22 to 28¢.

There might even be jokes, as during a revolution in Iberia:

WANTED—NEW KING FOR SPAIN

NO BLANKET NEEDED

A blanket was the only equipment required in most camps. The operator furnished the straw for the bunkhouse beds. A man taking a job from a job shark was entitled to store his bedroll and any other gear he chose with the agent until he was ready to take off for camp. Slave shops usually had storerooms with encased bins where loggers left their "turkeys"; if by chance a roll was free of lice when it went on deposit, it was sure not to be similarly unencumbered when withdrawn.

Down along the old skid roads one might see leering from dirty windows the sign of the grinning cat on the wood shoe: the symbol of sabotage, and of the Wobblies, formally called the Industrial Workers of the World—an amalgam of violence and idealism fused by the pressure of intolerable working conditions in an industry yielding enormous profits.

There was war in the woods from 1900 to 1920 as the I.W.W. and other unions fought the employers and terrorized the professionally timid editorialists in milltown papers. But out of the struggle came better conditions (and higher lumber prices) and an industry no longer feudal, or anarchic, but ready to face the more subtle problems of production and marketing and conservation of the twentieth century.

The FORESTS
. . . . . . now

"**N**OT FOR US, nor for our children, but for our grandchildren," said Frederick Weyerhaeuser, the tough, far-seeing German immigrant, greatest lumberman of them all, when he bought 900,000 acres of Northwest timber from his St. Paul neighbor, Jim Hill, greatest railroad builder of them all.

It was a statement at sixes and sevens with the spirit of the times, a spirit best expressed by the battle cry of most lumbermen, "Cut and Get Out." But it has proved understatement. The grandsons of Frederick Weyerhaeuser and their sons are working on the original Weyerhaeuser holdings now, and the end of the forest and the family is beyond sight over the horizon. They plan an endless cycle of cutting and growing, growing and cutting, with a new forest to be available on the same old grounds every century.

Once upon a time, and not a long time ago, the reformers looked only to the government for the salvation of the forests. The idea that a timber baron might see the necessity of preserving his barony by regulating the cut and encouraging regrowth seemed as chimerical as a rocket flight to the moon, or social security. Timber beasts ate timber, and that was that; you could no more re-strain their appetites than you could housebreak a pig. Thus, conventional wisdom.

Self-interest is an efficient educator. Those knowledgeable enough to acquire vast holdings were intelligent enough, in time, to realize that it might be more to their interest to farm the forest than to mine it. Except for the government, the Weyerhaeusers owned the most stumpage in the Pacific Northwest; there is no one, not even excepting the government, who manages forests better.

The secret of good forestry in the Pacific Northwest is size. Saws are efficient. There is no way for a small operator to space his cutting over the growing cycle of a conifer and keep his fallers and his mills busy from the growth of his own land. Even if a small operator holds his cut-over land and encourages reforestation, he is forced to buy timber, or logs, on the open market while waiting for his own trees to mature, and such purchases erode profits.

The Weyerhaeuser Company owns some 3,400,000 acres of timber, of which 2,750,000 are in the Northwest. There are larger holders of acreage in the United States (International Paper has nearly 6,000,000 acres) but Weyer-haeuser's 60,000,000,000 board feet in Washington and Oregon add up to the richest single privately owned forest domain in the country. The seed stand of this barony was the 900,000 acres that founding father Frederick Weyerhaeuser purchased from Jim Hill at $6 an acre. Much of its growth in size and value was the result of the care, tender and otherwise, of an ascetic logging genius named George Long.

Long was a lean, stretch-necked man who looked more like a village minister than the boss of the world's most valuable single stand of timber. He was no dried daisy. When Long met a veritable specimen of the old species of lumberjack and that unsuspecting original decided to walk Long's city legs off on an inspection tour, the logger had no way of knowing that Long could outwalk a camel. After one such endeavor a frazzled, panting straw boss said, "Hell, you might as well expect to get sweat outa a soupbone." Whatever Long did was unexpected to strangers. Old-timers still tell of the occasion when he gazed severely at a hooting, howling motley of mill owners, all convention-drunk, and admonished them, "Log-gers, when you are sober I admire you. But when you're drunk, God damn you, I love you."

Long's assignment was to consolidate the Weyerhaeuser holdings. Since the original stands had come out of the government land grant to the Northern Pacific, which got alternate sections on each side of its track, the stumpage was scattered in a pattern described as "a checkerboard snake." By shrewd trading and some selling, along with judicious buying when all else failed, Long grouped the Weyerhaeuser land in lumps big enough for economic logging. He had a wonderful sense of what lumbermen call "logging chance"; he went into the game with the largest table stake; and he had the wonderful advantage of time.

Weyerhaeuser was in no hurry to start cutting. The value of his holdings went up as the other operators sugared off their stumpage. George Long let rivals who needed to cross Weyerhaeuser land to reach their own do so: the logging roads they built increased the value of Weyerhaeuser land. Long and his masters were willing to wait, and they might be waiting yet had it not been for Theodore Roosevelt and the Panama Canal.

Teddy Roosevelt's advocacy of conservation was so strenuous that many a lesser holder of stumpage decided he had better cut before being embalmed in legislation. As other men cut, the Weyerhaeuser holdings rose still further in value. This did not escape notice of the assessor. So, when another of President Theodore Roosevelt's dreams came true, and the Panama Canal bisected the hemisphere and led to a fifty-per-cent drop in freight rates for lumber, Long decided it was time for the Weyerhaeusers to start cutting timber, but not Weyerhaeuser timber. He created a combination under which the Weyerhaeuser interests built a mill at Snohomish but purchased logs to saw from other operators. The experiment proved profitable. Only then did the "Big W" begin cutting, with deliberate care, its own forests.

Like a few other large operators, Weyerhaeuser has made it a policy to retain its cut-over land and let the forest grow back. About half of the Weyerhaeuser holdings in the Northwest at present are mature virgin timber, the bulk of it in Oregon. The rest consists of second growth not yet large enough to harvest.

The crucial problem for timber companies that want to stay in business is to space out the reaping of wild forest most profitably across the years until the tame second growth is ready for the saws and chippers. For Weyerhaeuser the reborn forests will begin maturing early in the twenty-first century. A team of some 175 graduate foresters gather data on which Weyerhaeuser's forest-management people base the allowable annual cut. Economists estimate (with the aid of the Stanford Research Bureau) the company's timber needs in the foreseeable future; the foresters determine the number and size of trees required to meet the needs, the period of time it will take to grow the trees, the inventory of all stands allocated to the various Weyerhaeuser processing centers. On the basis of these estimates, Weyerhaeuser has been taking between 1,000,000,000 and 1,300,000,000 board feet from its own holdings each year. If the company is called on to supply more lumber than this, it buys logs on the open market from other owners of stumpage, or bids for the right to harvest National Forest land.

On clear days when the winter snows lie on the western mountains a patchwork of white stands out against the greenish black of the conifer forest. These are logged-off areas, clear-cut, and in their outline you can make out the mighty geometry of modern logging.

No sight is more appalling to the amateur conservationist than clear-cut forest land. The tin-hatted loggers with their snarling chain saws have taken every tree; the great cats have snaked the logs to yarding areas; improbable machines have juggled and stacked the carcasses on flatcars or trucks, or pushed them into the water to be herded into floating corrals for convoy to the saws. On the deserted battlefield where the forest fell, the raw stumps of amputated trees darken under the unfamiliar sun, then are charred and blackened as left-over slash is burned by a controlled fire. This seems tree butchery at its most flagrant, but it is not.

The Douglas fir, basic tree of the northwest, is intolerant of shade. Seedlings will not mature under the pall of other trees. By nature a Douglas fir forest gradually gives way to a climax forest of hemlock and cedar, trees that can grow in the shade of other trees. Only after fire sweeps away the climax forest do the Douglas fir seeds fall on open ground, and a new stand of firs appears and grows to maturity. Clear-cutting is the forester's substitute for fire.

Where natural reseeding will not turn the reforestation trick, other methods are used. In the years when the conifers produce heavy crops, some cones are gathered and their germinal cargoes of seed removed and stored for use in the years—such as 1960—when the cone crop fails. A technique has recently been developed for treating the seed to make it less tasty to forest animals. This makes possible the reseeding of cut-over and burned land from the air. In 1960 the Weyerhaeuser Company alone scattered seed from helicopters over 15,000 acres; another 7700 acres were hand-planted with almost five million seedlings raised on nurseries.

In test-tube forests throughout the Northwest the forest geneticists— "foresters in white," they are sometimes called—are working to produce a race of super-trees. At Crown Zellerbach's Pacific Tree Farm, for example, a stand of 760 seedlings grafted from near-perfect firs is maturing and should probably bear their initial cone and seed crop somewhere between 1967 and 1970, from which the geneticists hope to develop Douglas firs with little taper, full diameter, and few limbs.

Should such an experiment actually produce a small stand of super-trees, it might be exploited as a source of seed through techniques of fertilization developed by Dr. John Duffield, the forest geneticist for the Industrial Forestry Association, and Dr. Eugene Steinbrenner, the forest-soils specialist at the Weyerhaeuser Forest Research Center. In 1955 they established an experimental forest in a small plot in the Yacolt burn area, which had been swept by a disastrous fire half a century earlier. Their experiments indicate that certain fertilizer treatments stimulate growth and a tremendous increase in cone and seed production.

In another experiment trees are being grown in a chamber that controls the weather. Here foresters can create a day in a tree's life that is only three hours long; here they can manipulate rain or the shock of temperature change; here may be determined what constellations of natural circumstances produce optimum growth or severe injury. In one recent experiment a seedling's annual growth cycle was compressed into sixty days.

Scientists at the University of Washington's College of Forestry, under federal sponsorship, are conducting long-range experiments on tree nutrition in the field. The foresters have developed an unusual apparatus known as a tension lysimeter, which collects liquids moving through soil profiles at varying layers in the ground, thus enabling the scientists to follow the path of nutrients down through the root zone. Dr. Stanley Gessel, who is in charge of this project, predicts that under the right conditions it should be possible to double the rate of tree growth.

Radioactive tracer elements are also used to track down forest enemies, such as microscopic insects. Researchers for pulp mills have been injecting young trees with radioactive carbon to study nutrient distribution and chemical utilization within the complex internal system of trees. They wait for the carbon to circulate, then cut down the trees and study tagged components from the bark, lignin, cellulose, and hemi-cellulose that make up the tree. This work may lead to the discovery of—among other things—commercial uses for lignin, the most abundant waste from paper and cardboard production. Lignin remains a considerable mystery to chemists in spite of years of intensive research. It is the brown binder that holds together the white cellulose fibers of wood; chemists describe it as a carbohydrate, aromatic in nature, made of benzine rings with a three-carbon chain attached. Though some uses have been found for lignin as a binder for highway blacktopping, as a paste for laying linoleum, as vanillin flavoring for candy and pastry, pulp mills must still dispose of from one million to two million tons of waste lignin each year. A fortune awaits the discoverer of a process that will permit its utilization.

Over the past several years, one phase of research at Weyerhaeuser has concentrated on the development of commercial uses for Douglas fir bark—an enterprise troubling to those of us who comb the beach for bark, or fisherman's coal as it sometimes is called, in the belief that there is no fire so satisfying, not even an alder fire, as that provided by a fireplace full of salt-cured bark. So far the scientists have not found uses for all the available bark, but the research continues. One of their most interesting achievements was the derivation from bark of a useful chemical, quercetin, now in commercial production for pharmaceutical and chemical use. Quercetin has been known for about a century; it is found in many plants and flowers and, until replaced by synthetics, was extracted for its dyeing qualities and for use as an additive to prevent such products as rubber, plastics, petroleum, insecticides, animal feeds, and vegetable and animal oils from spoiling or deteriorating when in contact with air. Quercetin has a broad range of ultraviolet absorptivity, and when used in certain other products prevents spoilage caused by exposure to ultraviolet light. Historians are charmed by its derivation from western conifers, since quercetin is in a family of compounds which are said to work together with Vitamin C in preventing and curing scurvy; its production from bark recalls the days when explorers and fur-traders on landing on the Northwest Coast immediately brewed from the green tips of evergreens that anti-scurvy specific, spruce beer.

Other areas of research in the woods range from ways to use helicopters in logging to the tape-recording of insects eating trees, and the development of painless traps for bears. George Schroeder, chief forester for Crown Zellerbach, predicts that helicopters will be accepted logging equipment by the end of the decade. Donald Allen, who is in charge of forest entomology for Oregon's State Forest Research Center, lugs a high-fidelity tape recorder into the forest, strips away bark on a fir log, staples some thin plastic over the exposed wood, attaches a tiny microphone to the plastic, and records the magnified sound of Douglas fir bark beetles as they munch away. From the data he is gathering Allen hopes to find a way of protecting the living trees against one of their smallest but most dangerous enemies.

One of the largest destroyers of trees is the black bear. Foresters estimate that bears now destroy a hundred times more trees in the Northwest than fire. Bears love the sapwood in young trees, particularly in the early spring, when the bears come out of hibernation and little food is available. A bear in a stand of ten to thirty-year-old second growth moves from tree to tree, stripping off the bark to get at the cambium layer, which is rich in starches and sugars. A single bear may kill a thousand trees a season. Several large companies have hired professional bear killers, the most famed of whom is Bill Hulet of Aberdeen, Washington, a former deputy sheriff and whisky peddler who claims to have killed more bears than any man who ever lived. Others trap the bears, and Jack Aldrich, a professional trapper from Castle Rock, Washington, has devised a new snare for bear, which has the advantage of being more efficient and less crippling than the traditional thirty-five-pound snap-jaw trap. Aldrich has also developed a sleepy-time spear—a long wooden tube full of tranquilizer with a syringe needle that can be released by a spring. He uses it to pacify snared bears so they can be loaded into cages and carried to less vulnerable areas to be turned loose.

Though new uses are continually being found for wood, and new ways developed to stimulate the growth of trees, though the tame forest is replacing the wild and the pattern of reforestation is passing from the determination of

The mighty geometry of modern logging stands out on the forested shoulders of Mount Rainier. Patches, linked by logging roads, have been clear cut, every tree removed. The surrounding forest facilitates natural reseeding.

Logging, first industry of the Pacific Northwest, has evolved from a primitive hand-to-hand combat by a man armed with only an ax or saw against a tree perhaps fifteen feet thick, into a complex industrial-agricultural operation. But some phases of the industry have changed little. Boom-men still leap from log to log as they tend the rafted raw material awaiting the blades and chippers of sawmills and pulpmills.

RAY ATKESON

Two loggers attack a giant fir with power saws on Vancouver Island, British Columbia.

This modern logging machine can wield a twenty-foot log as a conductor might a baton.

Aerial view of Shelton, Washington. Logs are assembled in Oakland Bay, where the Rayonier Company has a pulpmill and the Simpson Company a sawmill and plywood plant. The Olympics rise in the background.

Jets of water under high pressure rip the bark off logs as they are hauled into a mill.

A technician with a machine unrolls a Douglas fir into a sheet for plywood.

nature to that of man, the basic resource of today's lumbermen remains nature's forest.

No company comes close to monopolizing the production of lumber or pulp, not even mighty Weyerhaeuser. Though it is the largest sawyer of boards, the Big W's share of the national lumber market is only four per cent; of national pulp production, six per cent. In the Northwest, where the bulk of its holdings lies, Weyerhaeuser acreage is less than one-twelfth of that in government-held timberland.

The largest share of the federal forest land is controlled by the Department of Agriculture in the National Forests, the rest by the Department of Interior in the National Parks. The Forest Service is dedicated to a multiple use of its lands for water storage, recreation, and logging; opponents say the Forest Service considers that its prime function is to provide public logs at reasonable prices for private mills. The Park Service is increasingly dedicated to the wilderness concept, which calls for the preservation of the land in primeval purity with the threads of the wilderness pattern unbroken; opponents say the Park Service considers that its prime function is to lock up the land so tightly that citizens undevoted to tent and knapsack cannot look closely at their national heritage.

The king-of-the-mountain free-for-all among the big operators, the factions within the federal government, the little operators, the state governments, and various other governmental units controlling forest lands is the most fascinating and obscure politico-economic struggle in the Northwest. But it is significant that all parties involved feel obliged to pay formal obeisance before the new god of sustained yield. The shibboleth of "Cut and Get Out" is no longer heard. No experienced puntman would put long odds on any of the contestants against the rest of the field in the struggle for control of the forests; but the odds are increasingly favorable that the forests themselves will survive the struggle.

The LAND
......then

THE INDIANS of the Pacific Northwest planted nothing. Not for them the corn seed fertilized by the rotting fish. Their economy was purely extractive. They hunted deer and elk, they snared birds and rabbits, they dug wild camas roots and clams, they gathered oysters and berries, they caught fish with gear that was durable, complex, and ingenious, they put out into the open ocean in their high-prowed canoes to hunt otters, seals, and whales; but they did not farm. The sea and the forest and the untilled plains provided them with such bounty that some tribes, to invest it, devised the complex gift ceremony of the potlatch: a man receiving a gift had, in time, to give the donor a larger one, or be shamed. They had the leisure to develop a powerful art form; carving infused their lives. They had neither knowledge of nor need for agriculture. Not until the white men came was the soil broken.

The Spaniards, accustomed to bending both land and Indians to farming, carried seeds with them from Mexico. The colonies they planted at Nootka and Neah Bay withered before the garden patches could grow into haciendas.

A few of the English sea captains trading regularly on the Northwest Coast grew potatoes and peas in plots beside their factories, as they termed the warehouses in which furs were stored, but they undertook no serious gardening. Captain Vancouver, when exploring Puget Sound, cited the agricultural possibilties of his discovery but did not exploit them.

In the spring of 1810 Nathan Winship of the Boston Winships came in the *Albatross* to the lower Columbia. He landed in the vicinity of modern Rainier, and built, at Fanny's Bottom, a two-story log house; he planted a garden of grain and vegetables, and staked out some hogs and goats. The spring floods washed out this first American farm in the Northwest, and soon afterward the Indians chased out Winship.

John Jacob Astor's more ambitious plans for the Northwest Coast included not only the harvesting of furs but the raising of livestock and other foodstuffs for export to the Russians at New Archangel. The men of the American Fur Company arrived ready for agriculture. But when the old mountain hands of the North West Company took over Astoria, they had no stomach for commercial farming; the most they would deign to do was raise a few delicacies for their own tables. Not until 1824, when Governor George Simpson of Hudson's Bay decreed that Company posts raise their own food or go hungry, was the soil seriously worked.

Fort Vancouver on the Columbia was chosen partially for its agricultural possibilities, and a 300-acre portion of the upper prairie was broken by the plow at about the same time that work started on the buildings. In 1825 there were planted potatoes, peas, beans, and perhaps a few leaf vegetables. With satisfaction Chief Factor John McLoughlin noted the harvest that first year: 900 barrels of potatoes and nearly ten bushels of peas. During the next decade the company expanded its farming operations. McLoughlin encouraged retired employees to take farmland, particularly south of the Columbia, where he feared an influx of American settlers, but he did his best to make sure the farmers had no place to sell produce or fill their needs other than the company store.

In the fall of 1834 there appeared at the gates of Fort Vancouver a pair of Americans, one shaking with malaria, the other shaken by anger. The sick man was Hall Jackson Kelley, the founder (and often sole member) of the American Society for Encouraging the Settlement of Oregon Territory. As odd an Irishman as Boston has yet produced, Kelley had fallen in love with the Oregon country from across the continent. In broadside and pamphlet, from platform and street corner, Kelley proclaimed Oregon American and labeled the British in general and the Hudson's Bay Company in particular as usurpers; he propagandized for United States aid to emigrants, whose settlement in Oregon would, he argued, decide the issue. It was Kelley who had interested Nathaniel Wyeth in the idea of establishing a commercial empire on the Columbia. When Wyeth, who was unconventional enough to pay Kelley heed but not fool enough to accept him as prophet, realized the Irishman was a crank and brushed him off, Kelley set out independently for Oregon. After a series of tragicomic misadventures en route to his promised land, Kelley encountered near San Diego Ewing Young, a paladin among American mountain men.

This Young was old in the tough life of the pre-pioneer. Born in Tennessee, Young had ridden the wave of the frontier westward; he had trapped beaver, he had fought Apaches, and with a youth named Kit Carson in tow he had packed across the Mojave Desert, emerging in California. Itching for wealth, Young had tried exporting Mexican mules to Missouri; it didn't work. Young went back to trapping, swinging up into the southern Oregon country, then working his way down to San Diego, where he considered settling down in the miller's trade. Before his chance meeting there with Hall Kelley, the Tennessee trapper had gone so far as to order millstones.

Kelley, who had the gall of a telephone sales solicitor, made his customary pitch about the marvels of the Oregon country; he was unfazed by the fact that he had never been there and that Young had just returned. Here was a contest: the convinced salesman versus the experienced skeptic. Young held out and Kelley, shrugging off yet another apparent defeat, started north alone. But the promotion patter plus Young's instinct for the frontier eventually caused the Tennessean to change his mind; he abandoned the millstones, rounded up a half-dozen companions, bought some horses, and started north. By chance Young's party caught up with Kelley near San Francisco, and they joined forces.

En route north, the Americans fell in briefly with a band of horse thieves, whose atrocities against the Indians made the rest of their journey more than normally dangerous, and who eventually departed with a considerable portion of Young's livestock. Nor was that the worst of it. The Mexican authorities in California sent word to Factor McLoughlin at Fort Vancouver, wrongly identifying Young as the boss horse thief.

So it was that when Young and Kelley, the latter racked by malaria, arrived at the Hudson's Bay Company fort on the Columbia, McLoughlin turned Young away as a thief. The factor recognized and loathed Kelley as an alien jingoist and professional slanderer of the Hudson's Bay Company. Though Kelley made altruism no easier by demanding his rights as "an American on American soil," McLoughlin felt he could not deny aid to a sick man. He provided Kelley with shelter and food, though he kept his guest so far below the salt that Kelley did not get to the gentleman's table at all; instead he was served his food in quarters, which quarters he later described as a mean lean-to previously used for dressing out fish and fowl. There Kelley stayed, grousing continuously, the most unwelcome of guests, denied the hospitality for which Fort Vancouver was famed, visited

Vancouver in 1854. A picture drawn by Gustavus Sohon which appears in Volume XII of the War Departments Reports of Explorations and Surveys, to Ascertain the Most Practicable and Economic Route for a Railroad from the Mississippi River to the Pacific Ocean. *The Hudson's Bay Company stockade appears in the right center, with the Columbia beyond. The village has grown up between the stockade and the military barracks behind the parade ground under the flag.*

Symbol of the arid open spaces was the Grand Coulee.
Carved by the Columbia when the great river was rerouted
by a glacier during the Ice Age, the coulee was left high
and dry when the river returned to its old channel. This is
the way it looked to the Isaac Stevens party in 1854.

"We are beyond," wrote Maude Kraymer to her cousin
after crossing the prairie in a stagecoach. "We tell time by
the sun and measure the months in baths. I would wish I
were home if getting there did not mean going back over
those choking prairies."

This copy of a photograph of a covered wagon train was found among the files of Asahel Curtis, a pioneer photographer in the state of Washington, but it was not taken by him originally. Whether it is a copy of a picture actually taken in the days of the wagon trains, or merely a copy of a movie still, is uncertain. It does reflect the feeling of distance and dryness which was common to the pioneer experience.

Lonely men who had longed for land of their own built houses from the rocks of their fields, broke the plains with team and plow, and planted wheat and corn.

While first crops did well, they exhausted the stored-up surface moisture of the plains, and after a few good years many farms dried up. Pioneers hung on as long as they could, but eastern Washington and Oregon are dotted with empty farmhouses, tombstones for dreams that died.

Not until the railroads reached the Northwest did the land begin to fill. Once steel was laid, the railroads had to stimulate immigration so there would be people to raise crops and cut lumber for the lines to haul. The coming of the Great Northern in 1892 led to the settlement and eventual irrigation of the land around Wenatchee. Some of the pioneers lived in tents, others in wanigans—shanties on wheels.

Little towns, such as Two Rivers, Washington, sprang up to sell supplies to the farmers and to store their wheat until it could be sent to the elevators to await shipment down the river or over the mountains.

*Paddlewheel steamers thrashed up the broad Columbia,
competing with freight trains for the right to haul grain.*

OPPOSITE: *The ships of the world fought their way across the Columbia bar or around Cape Flattery and down the Strait of Juan de Fuca to Puget Sound to pick up the golden cargoes of wheat. Here the four-masted schooner* Commodore, *veteran of the wheat fleet, fights heavy seas off Tatoosh.*

The decline of dry-farming, coupled with the opening of the Panama Canal and the rise of the steamers, meant the end of the white-winged wheat fleet. Most were retired, but some were deliberately wrecked. Here is the British Glenesslin *on the beach at Neahkanie on the Oregon coast, victim of one of the strangest wrecks in maritime history. On October 1, 1913, her captain ordered full sail, set a course toward land, and ordered no one to change course on pain of being charged with mutiny. Then he drank himself into a stupor while his ship ran onto the coast in broad daylight. She was a total loss but all hands were saved.*

AL MON

The dark, fertile earth of a Willamette Valley field reveals the delicate newly sprouted grain, while beyond sweeps the space of last season's harvested field.

only rarely by such of his landsmen as happened to pass through the Columbia country. Only once, for instance, was he called upon by his old protégé, Nathaniel Wyeth. When Kelley was healthy enough to be gone, McLoughlin arranged passage for him to Hawaii and loaned him thirty-five dollars spending money, which McLoughlin did not expect to see again, nor did he.

Meanwhile the embittered Ewing Young had taken his suspect horses south of the Columbia, to cultivate his wheat crops and his grudge against the Company. He was not alone. Most of the other settlers in the area were retired French-Canadian employees of the Company, who had taken Indian women as wives and preferred to live out their years in the Northwest. They owed some loyalty to Hudson's Bay Company, but they were not beyond the natural frustrations of farmers forced to buy their supplies from and sell their crops to a company store.

Also to the area at this time came the Methodist missionary Jason Lee, who had been dispatched across the country in answer to what came to be known as "the cry from Macedonia," a plea by "Flathead" Indians, who coveted either salvation or white magic, and asked someone to teach them. En route west, Jason Lee changed destinations. He decided to concentrate his attentions on the more easily accessible souls in the Willamette valley rather than to follow the migratory tribes across Colorado, Wyoming, and Montana. McLoughlin encouraged the burly divine to settle south of the Columbia, partly because he felt the minister's presence would be a good influence on the French Canadians, their Indian consorts, and their children, partly because he was doing his best to confine Americans to the areas for which the British had the least claim to possession when the boundaries were ultimately drawn.

The juxtaposition of these two sturdy, stubborn men, Ewing Young and Jason Lee, was an ironic tangling of two main lines of American expansion. Young, the trapper and mountain man, the restless pursuer of the frontier, a lone wolf, his citizenship and his patriotism light baggage; and Lee, farm-bred, converted at a backwoods meeting, educated late, determined to save souls for Christ and Oregon for the Unitd States, a man cast westward by the wave of revivalism then sweeping the East, devout, puritanical, inflexible, intolerant, and patriotic.

Like other settlers, Ewing Young had no ready market for his wheat other than the Company warehouse, and in his bitterness after McLoughlin dismissed him as a horse thief he refused to darken the gate of Fort Vancouver with his shadow. So, with a partner, he rigged up a still out of a copper salmon-pickling kettle abandoned by the Wyeth men, and set about turning grain into a more easily marketable commodity.

There were those who looked on Young's improvised still as the coming of civilization to the Willamette Valley. Not so Jason Lee. He responded by organizing a Temperance Society (like Young's moonshine a pioneer thing of its kind in the area), but neither argument nor written petition was enough to bring about the discontinuance of distillation.

Factor McLoughlin, like Lee a teetotaller, was likewise disturbed by the existence in his satrapy of a supply of alcohol beyond his control. (He quarreled, for instance, with a Church of England clergyman who had been sent to the fort, whom he felt to be too liberal with the brandy when pouring toasts.) So when an American, William Slacum, who claimed to be a businessman but whom McLoughlin correctly guessed to be a special agent of President Andrew Jackson, came by Fort Vancouver in the summer of 1836, McLoughlin suggested that it would be to Oregon's benefit if Slacum could persuade his countrymen to get out of the whisky business. Slacum agreed to try. Remarkably, he succeeded.

Out of the negotiations over hard liquor grew a plan for an alternate use of the Willamette grain: it would be fed to cattle. Since there were few cattle in the area, and those the property of Hudson's Bay Company, which would not sell its herd, it was decided that Spanish cattle should be purchased in California and driven north. The plan was ambitious and risky: it required money, a good eye for cattle, some diplomacy in negotiating with the Mexican officials, experience on the trail. There was a general drawing together of rival factions in the face of the challenge: Jason Lee backed the nomination of Young as the leader of the expedition, McLoughlin put up some of the money needed to purchase the herd, Slacum arranged free passage to California on a government ship. In spite of slow bureaucrats, high water, and Indians, Young brought the cattle through. Their presence in the Willamette valley did much to make farming profitable and the land attractive. The cattle drive was one of the turning points in the settlement of the country.

While Young was chivvying the gaunt California longhorns north from the Imperial Valley, a party of missionaries was toiling westward across the plains with a yet more precious addition to life in the Northwest—Marcus Whitman's lovely wife Narcissa and Henry Spalding's wife Eliza, dark-haired and dour.

Though by no means the first white women to reach the Northwest (Captain Charles Barkley had brought his young bride in 1787; Donald McTavish of the Nor'westers had imported a doxy from Portsmouth to Astoria in 1814; and there were a number of white women at Fort Vancouver who had arrived by sea), Narcissa and Eliza were the first white women to make it across the Rockies and the first to take residence in the land between the Rockies and the Cascades. Just as Young's cattle were to play a continuing role in the history of the lower Columbia country, so too were the missionary women in the lands upriver. Their presence showed the overland journey to be less than impossible. Others followed.

By the time Ewing Young made his last great contribution to the development of the Pacific Northwest by dying intestate in 1841, there were some 150 Americans and between 700 and 800 Canadians and mixed-breeds in the Oregon country. But there was no law other than moral suasion and the right of self-defense. Young was the most well-to-do American on the Willamette, and his claim with its herd of fat cattle was a rich prize. He had no known heirs and left no will. In a land innocent of written law because its ownership remained in dispute between Britain and the United States, no one could be sure what would happen to the acres Young had fenced and the herd he had fattened.

Jason Lee, the most influential of the Americans, used the occasion of Young's funeral to press for the organization of a de facto government. Those assembled for the interment at first indicated agreement to setting up a body of officials that included a governor, road commissioners, and an overseer of the poor. Second thoughts prevailed, however, and at a second meeting on the day after Young's burial the settlers, with more of the Canadians in attendance, trimmed down the table of organization to a judge with probate powers, a clerk, a sheriff, and a trio of constables. Dr. Ira L. Babcock, a lay member of the Lee Mission, was chosen judge and agreed, pending the creation of a local body of law, to follow the New York State laws, a copy of which was available.

This fell far short of real government. The judge's power extended no further than the consent of those on whom he sought to impose a decision. (The provisional court was able to probate Young's estate, sold the property, and held the money in trust; some years later, when it was determined that Young had a son in the East, the court turned the money over to him.) There were valid reasons why men should hesitate to encourage the formation of a government, no matter how inconvenient the lack of laws. The Canadians felt that any government taking control south of the Columbia would be dominated by the Americans, and that if the United States gained possession the Canadians' right to own property they had settled would come into question. Many American settlers had similar fears: if Oregon belonged to the United States might not all land, including that developed by the settlers, be considered part of the public domain and open for claim by newcomers? There were also men who had come to the Oregon country because it was beyond the law and who aimed to keep it that way.

Nevertheless the establishment of the probate court to handle Young's estate was the first step toward government. It was followed by the so-called wolf meetings, at which the settlers gathered to set bounties on predators decimating the flocks and herds; the bounties were to be paid out of voluntary contributions, not taxes. By 1843 the Americans agreed to the establishment of a provisional government, with a legislature, courts, and a three-man committee to take the place of a governor. This triumvirate was inefficient enough to convince the settlers within two years that it would be better to put power in the hands of one man, a provisional governor; that same year, 1845, McLoughlin decided that the Hudson's Bay Company could cooperate with the provisional government, and the weight of its law was extended north of the Columbia.

In the meantime the Americans had continued to pour across the mountain barrier. Missionaries and politicians and cranks like Hall Kelley called the attention of the folks back east to the land available in the West. Patriotism moved some to come here, restlessness others, religion still others; some fled families or the law or failure; some were curious and footloose. But above all they did venture to the West because, as the mountaineers say, it was there. The bands and parties were soon replaced by the wagon trains that moved under semi-military discipline. They deepened and broadened the old trails through the mountains; the wheels of their wagons and the hoofs of their oxen and horses broke through the springy sod of the plains so that after the first few years the trip was a hell of dust. Their foragers enraged the Indians by assaults on the buffalo and antelope that were the staff of life to the tribes of the plains. The travelers died of drowning and heat, of cholera and arrow, of starvation; some died of sheer frustration. But the tide of westward migration continued to rise, and every year more people got here.

Factor McLoughlin at Fort Vancouver managed to divert most of the Americans south of the Columbia, but not only did the flow of immigrants wash out the Canadian majority in the fort area but, in their passage westward, they disrupted trapping and hunting in much of the area between the Columbia and the Fraser. The Hudson's Bay Company was forced to concentrate on lands farther north; it withdrew its headquarters from Fort Vancouver to Fort Victoria across the Strait of Juan de Fuca. In 1845 the first of the arriving flood of Americans ignored McLoughlin's pointed suggestions that they would do better across the Columbia and went north to the southern reaches of Puget Sound. It was not pure patriotism that drove this party north to settle alongside the Hudson's Bay Company's subsidiary agricultural holdings at Nisqually; one of the leaders of the party was a Negro, George Bush, and the Americans along the Willamette were hostile to Negroes. But that a small group of Americans could defy the clear wishes of the Company was deeply significant.

Only a year later, England decided that the lands under joint occupancy south of the Fraser were not worth a war with the United States. President Polk retreated from the extravagance of the "54-40 or fight" position, under which

OPPOSITE: *Mount Hood, Oregon, reflected in the waters of Trillium Lake and framed in vine maple leaves.*

RAY ATKESON

96

In Mount Rainier National Park, Washington, a spectacular scenic highway sweeps along the side of Sunrise Ridge toward Mount Rainier, "The Monarch of the Northwest." The Emmons Glacier pours down the slopes of the great mountain for several miles from its 14,410-foot crest.

OPPOSITE: *Rain forest, Olympic Peninsula, Washington.*

RAY ATKES

Wheatfield, eastern Oregon.

the United States claimed everything up to Russian America. The boundary following the 49th parallel to salt water was agreed upon.

Even after the Oregon country became American, the laws of the United States were not extended to it. The settlers were left in a state of legal limbo. Congress, entangled in the controversy over whether new areas should permit slavery, simply delayed recognizing Oregon as a territory until death again played a decisive part.

On November 29, 1847, the Cayuse Indians attacked the Whitman mission at Waiilatpu, "the place of the rye grass," in the broad valley of the Walla Walla. They killed fourteen persons, including Marcus and Narcissa Whitman.

The tragedy of the Whitmans was a classic American tragedy. It has been enacted, in varying forms, many times in our history. It grew out of grace, bravery, and fine intentions; out of willingness to endure hardship and of the eager embrace of personal sacrifice; out of a dedication to the saving of souls; out of a conviction—smug but deep-rooted—of a personal duty to make more like the American's own the condition of an alien people far from convinced that they needed change. The reluctance of the recipient peoples only spiced the challenge. There were in Marcus and Narcissa Whitman a peculiarly American greatness, an idealism and determination, and what seems to another age a willful wrong-headedness in dealing with the peoples they so sincerely sought to help.

The fatal flaw in the Whitman approach was their assumption that the best thing that could happen to an Indian was to become a white man. They did their utter best, traveling beyond the frontiers of exhaustion, to bestow upon the tribes of the interior the blessings of Christianity, responsible government, agriculture, the written word, mathematics, carpentry, and New England morality. If this dose of civilization proved too much for the Indians to take at a gulp, the Whitmans were prepared to be understanding, but firm. A Son of God must swallow what was good for him.

As for the Indians, they were not reluctant to learn things from the white man, whose command of superior power, or technique, or magic, they recognized and feared and coveted. But, being human, the Indians wanted not abrupt change but enrichment; they wanted to pick and choose from among the possibilities offered by the whites; they wanted to learn, as Indians. And they did not wholly admire the newcomers to their country. Through their eyes, the bearded, land-fencing foreigner seemed contradictory indeed. He preached peace, but killed for odd and contradictory reasons. He spoke of the rights of property, but took the land of the Indians. He urged the tribal chiefs, whose powers were limited in their village democracies, to punish tribesmen who violated the rules of the whites, and yet he claimed that whites in the Oregon country were powerless to punish their skin brothers in California for abuse of an Indian chief's son. He spoke of Universal Law descending from a Father of All, but when the whites got smallpox few died and when the Indians got smallpox whole villages died. The Whitmans, for example, claimed to know God as a father and to speak in his name: why then had their two-year-old daughter drowned in a creek at Waiilatpu? And what of "Father" Whitman, six feet three and powerful as a bear, who, when slapped in the face by a brave, with shuddering self-control slowly turned his other cheek? Or "Mother" Whitman who talked of the comforting love of God but was sometimes seen crying in corners?

And always more and more white men filing down out of the mountain passes, their women with them now, coming into the land and eying the sweet meadows and building cabins and fencing off the water.

They dreamed different dreams, the aborigines and the settlers, and the bridge between their cultures was too frail. A disgruntled band of Cayuses decided co-existence was a losing game and determined to wipe out the mission at the place of the rye grass. They came asking for medicine and they attacked without warning. Fourteen died, including several children; but the horror that grasped and held the imagination of the nation was the murder of the Whitmans. For they were a couple clearly intent on doing good, identified with the best instincts of America: Marcus, minister and physician, proponent of national expansion, guide to settlers westering after land, savior of orphans, converter of the heathen; and Narcissa, golden-haired, full-bodied, husky-voiced, cultured—a memory of eastern life to the shaggy Western men. Joe Meek, the mountain man, looked at her and remembered he had not tasted bread for nine years.

Marcus Whitman was tomahawked by an Indian asking for medicine, then shot through the throat at close range and left to die slowly. His thirty-five-year-old wife was shot in the chest when she opened the plank door of the mission to look for help, shot again when being carried from the building under a pledge of safe conduct. After she was dead one of the Cayuses held her upright and whipped her face.

Reaction to the atrocity was immediate. The power was there and the power was used. The provisional government of Oregon dispatched volunteers to bring in the murderers. They were caught and—most horrible of fates for a Northwest Indian—hanged.

A delegation under Joe Meek, the mountain man who happened to be related to the First Lady, galloped east to tell President Polk of the massacre. After a desperate journey Meek arrived in Washington in grimy buckskins and, brevetting himself "Envoy Extraordinary and Minister Plenipotentiary from the Republic of Oregon to the Court of the United States," presented a petition asking for the protection of American law and arms. Enabling legislation passed Congress in

August 1848, and on March 3, 1849 a day before President Polk turned over the reigns of government to Zachary Taylor, the territorial government was declared to be in operation. This gave the United States Army direct responsibility for pacifying the Indian country. There would be more uprisings—the final one the great futile stand of the Nez Percés under Chief Joseph—but the fate of the inter-mountain country was determined, as that of the coastal strip had been long before. It would be made safe for settlement.

The Whitmans had come West to win souls for Christ. In death they won the Inland Empire for the American settlers of their generation.

Gold strikes in the eastern part of the Oregon Territory following the California rush drew prospectors into the interior. Some stayed there to farm after the strikes were exhausted. The land was fruitful but the markets far away. Population growth was slow until the railroads came, opening the markets of the Midwest to the crops that could be raised on the rich, rolling hills of central Washington and Oregon and to lumber from the fir and pine forest that bristled on the shoulders of the mountains; opening, too, a sure path to salt water and the waiting ships.

The Northern Pacific was the first railroad across the continent to the Oregon country, coming hesitantly, its periods of construction matching the boom-and-bust fluctuations of the national economy. Then after the Northern Pacific, the Great Northern, creation of that burly figure out of folk lore, Jim Hill, the empire builder, described by a discerning but awe-struck biographer as "the barbed-wire, shaggy-headed, one-eyed old son of a bitch of western railroading."

The LAND
......*now*

SOME YEARS ago (1941, to be precise) my wife and I and our Belgian sheep dog Haj Vinca started down the Columbia in a kayak. We wet bottom in the shadow of the Grand Coulee dam, which was then the world's largest. We rode through the safe but exciting turbulence of the millrace, past the precisely distributed houses of the government town with their rich green lawns, and out into the barren rut the river had worn through the sagebrush bleakness of the Big Bend. The land above us was dry and dead; the river remained a thread of life that pulled us forward at some five miles an hour. Through the rubber hull of the boat we could feel its vitality pulsing against our legs.

That afternoon, with the memory of the mile-long concrete barrier still pressing on us, we rounded a curve and came on a hand-made water wheel turning slowly in an eddy. Its paddles slapped lazily against the stream, and tin cans attached to the frame dipped into the water, scooping up a quart or so, carrying it up, pouring it into a board trough, down which it ran to a vegetable patch that glowed green beside a sun-baked cabin.

The Grand Coulee dam, raising water from the great river and distributing

Marcus Whitman at the Waiïlatpu mission and the Catholic priests at Antanum Creek in Yakima, Washington, introduced irrigation to the dry lands east of the mountains. Private, state, and federal irrigation followed. But all were less than drops in the bucket compared to the Grand Coulee Reclamation Project. A mile-long dam, its spillway twice the height of Niagara, was thrown across the Columbia. A fraction of the power from its turbines is used to pump water from the 150-mile lake behind the dam into the enormous reservoir of the old Grand Coulee, the Ice-Age channel of the Columbia.

ABOVE: *A network of canals spreads across two million acres, turning wastes of sagebrush and tumbleweed into farmland. This is the West Canal, near Winchester, Washington, holding as much water as the Illinois or the Potomac.*

Enormous siphons carry the water from the Grand Coulee to the canals. The Soap Lake siphon, shown here. is nearly two and a half miles long and has an inside diameter of twenty-five feet.

RAY AT

AY ATKESON

The geometry of abundance—grain elevators near Klamath Falls, Oregon.

Grain harvest in eastern Washington.

Early Oregon radar? No, an old beef hoist on a ranch in southeastern Oregon.

AL MONNER

A cattle ranch on the Deschutes River in Oregon, another way of life redolent of the past.

Branding is done on the open range.

This blacksmith shop on Island Ranch near Burns, Oregon, was built around the turn of the century. Adjoining it is a wagon shop still stocked with parts enough to build wagons almost from the hoops up.

A cowboy's holiday may include trying to pick up prize money at a rodeo. The three biggest are the Pendleton Round-up, the Ellensburg Rodeo (below), and the Western Washington Fair at Puyallup.

Near Maupin spreads the Connolly Ranch, typical of the sheep-raising industry of Oregon. In winter, when temperatures drop below zero east of the mountains, sheep herders bring feed to the flock.

Shearing is a phase of sheep herding that has changed with the times. The clippers are now power-driven but the work still calls for strength, skill, and a flexible back.

The sacks of wool fleeces are piled to await shipment. An average sack holds more than three hundred pounds of wool.

The shorn sheep are moved from one corral to another by ranch hands. This picture could have been taken a hundred years ago.

There are towns that seem as change-less as paintings. Mrs. Maude Garrett is postmaster of Shaniko, and from her office door can look across the board-walk to the old hotel across the street and the few stores which serve widely scattered ranchers in central Oregon.

AL MO

Amid changes there are constants. A wonderful thing about life in the inter-mountain area of the Northwest is the intermingling of the old with the new. This Yakima Indian boy finds the best of two worlds.

it over an area embracing two million acres—and only a few miles downstream this wheel of driftwood, tin cans, and haywire watering a hermit's garden. These are the contrasts of the Northwest Corner, particularly of the inland country where a bearded rancher may fly his own plane to town for a Pioneer Day celebration; where the white cube rising against the horizon may be a grain elevator or an atomic power plant. The wooden water wheel above Box Canyon is now buried by the pond behind yet another dam, Chief Joseph—most beautiful of the shackles man has placed on the Columbia. But any trip through the inter-mountain country can furnish provocative juxtapositions:

An Indian boy in feather head-dress of a type that would have caused his ancestors to put on war paint sucks a bottle of pop at a festival staged by Indians to draw tourists into a land they once defended against the encroachments of the whites.

A Basque shepherd, recruited a few months earlier in Spain and flown to Oregon by jet, watches over a herd of sheep descended from merino stock originally stolen by Englishmen from the Spanish crown and taken to Australia.

A lean man in patched fatigues, chukka boots, and a red beret spends a morning shooting birds on the Columbia between Richland and Paso. This is no casual hunter but a scientist in the employ of the Atomic Energy Commission, whose job is to check the concentration of radioactivity in the birds that eat the insects that eat the minnows that feed on the plankton that grows in the river below the Hanford atomic works.

A procession of Indians in blue jeans, flannel shirts, and felt hats leads a string of ponies along a trail that follows the marching metal towers that carry the great looping lines of the Bonneville Power Administration.

Beside a thirty-foot-wide concrete ditch built to carry water across fifty miles of near desert a big, deserted farmhouse, vacant for half a century, stands like the ghost of a sentry amid acres of sunburnt land where a generation of farmers fought the dry volcanic soil for wheat, and lost.

The Columbia is ponded now for most of its length from Bonneville to the Canadian border. Hundreds of thousands of acres of the rich, dry soil have been brought under cultivation. Where once the dust devils danced, rainbows shimmer in the clouds of spray. The Grand Coulee itself—that great channel worn by the Columbia when the snout of an ice-age glacier blocked its original course, then left bone-dry when the river fell back into its original route—has filled with water raised by the great pumps at the dam and now serves as an equalizing reservoir; the coulee bed, where once the hoofs of long-horned cattle raised dust at each step, is lake bottom now.

In the rolling country around Walla Walla, where the ill-fated Whitmans showed the Indians how to plant seed, tractor-drawn gang plows, harrows, and drills cut and turn and pulverize the deep soil and measure out the seed grain. In late summer the combines sweep across the golden sea of wheat, each machine accompanied by its own cloud of chaff and straw and leaving in its wake the bags of grain. Fleets of trucks roll across the stubbled fields gathering in the bags and carrying them to the elevators and warehouses beside the railroad tracks or alongside the rivers, while in the legislatures and Congress the politicians from Puget Sound compete with those from downstream Columbia areas for transportation appropriations; the Puget Sound delegations seek funds for more and better tunnels through the Cascade barrier, and the Columbia contingent argues for improvements in river navigation. Across the years, the raising of wheat has changed more than the politics of wheat has.

The flow of water down the irrigation canals—first along the little ditches dug by the Catholic priests for the mission on Ahtanum Creek in the Yakima area and by the Whitmans in the valley of the Walla Walla; later along the deep cuts leading from storage dams built by the farmers' cooperatives and the privately owned utilities; finally along the concrete network of government siphons, pumps, reservoirs, and filters—has made possible the development of major new crops. There are the heavy-fruited apple orchards of the Yakima valley, the most productive in the country; the fields of sugar beets and peas for canning and freezing, the trellises festooned with hops, the mounds of potatoes high as a four-story building, the endless acres sharp with spearmint and peppermint.

But back up the valleys in the high rolling country where you feel the presence of the mountains, the old life lingers. The longhorns are long gone, replaced by plumper stock; the ranches remain, and the cowboys, angular men in wide-brimmed hats and high-heeled boots and blue jeans whitened with wear at seat, thighs and knees. On their rare nights in town, as they watch television across the tavern bar, the cowboys may still on occasion get into a fight with sheep herders, or they may get themselves killed racing back to the ranch—in pickup trucks; or risk a chunk of their wages to grubstake a buddy who has decided to turn prospector and set out into the pine forest with packhorse and Geiger counter.

Though the herds have increased so much in the years since Ewing Young first drove the Spanish longhorns up to the Willamette valley that now four million head are marketed annually in the Northwest, ranch life is not so different. Some of the spreads in southeastern Oregon, or the Tonasket valley of Washington, or the Willamette valley, now know the fourth generation of the founding family. These are rare, however, for the turnover among the early homesteaders was high. Still, were the founding patriarch to return, he would fit easily into the familiar routine of branding and haying, of shoeing the horses and tending the fences, though he would have to accustom himself perhaps to driving a truck instead of a wagon, and depending on the radio instead of the local Indians for weather misinformation.

Nor would the early shepherds find things uncomfortably different as they followed their willful, stupid, self-destructive, sharp-hoofed flocks through the high country. They would probably apply the same curses to the flocks that Joshua Shaw and his son did when they drove the first flock across the plains in 1844. Looking up through the thin night air at the stars and the occasional satellites, these men have more in common with the shepherds of a hundred years ago, or of two thousand years ago, than they do with the engineers down by the river at Coulee and Bonneville and Hanford.

Even in a land being rebuilt more to man's desire, climate and geology and occupation impose their imperatives. And as the omnipresence of water and the thrust of the fir and hemlock permeate the atmosphere west of the Cascades, so to the east does the clear, thin air, the biting contrast of season, the sweep of significant space, and the sharp, resin scent of the open forests of pine.

The CITIES

PORTLAND, Seattle, and Vancouver—these are the major cities of the Northwest. Each is a rail terminus, each a seaport, though none faces the open ocean. Portland straddles the Willamette at its juncture with the Columbia; Vancouver, the Fraser where it enters the Strait of Georgia; and Seattle, which rises from the hills between Puget Sound and Lake Washington, claims as its river the insignificant Duwamish. All are cities of the lumber and wheat trade, cities where freighters loll at the end of main street. All enjoy spectacular settings and glory in their neighboring mountains. Yet they are very different.

Portland is a New England town with gravity working for it; a conservative town, with much quiet beauty and most of its businessmen convinced that, sure as water flows down hill and the Columbia reaches the sea, the trade of the wheatlands will come to their doors.

Seattle, largest of the big three, with a 1960 population of 557,087, is the roughneck grown uneasily respectable, a middle-class city with its eye eternally on the main chance; a lumber town that gambled—and lost—on becoming the first great rail terminus of the Northwest but was able to parlay the Klondike and Alaska gold rushes into riches; a town that built ships for the first world war and bombers for the second, and is industriously tooling up for rockets.

Vancouver, with a population of 365,952 in the 1956 Canadian census, is the youngest, toughest, most energetic, most beautifully situated, and (Americans like to think) the most American of the three cities. It is growing faster than either of its rivals, and can boast the outstanding theater—the Queen Elizabeth—the two liveliest newspapers, the most cosmopolitan population, and the best fishing on the Pacific Coast.

Outstripped in size but with charms peculiar to themselves are Spokane, Tacoma, and Victoria, once pretenders for pre-eminence; and smaller towns such as New Westminster, Yakima, Corvallis, Wenatchee, Eugene, Bend, Walla Walla, Aberdeen, to name a few; some sleepy, some bustling; some, like Richland, as new as atomic power; others, like Oregon City or Snoqualmie, old-fashioned as falling water.

Portland is the oldest of the major cities, though at the time of its birth it was not without formidable rivals along the Columbia and the Willamette. Other contenders included Milwaukie, Oregon City, Rainier, St. Helens, and Milton City nearby, and at the mouth of the Columbia the durable Astoria and the ephemeral Pacific City, née Lancaster, a promoter's dream. This latter was on Baker's Bay on the north shore of the Columbia mouth, and it was in the great tradition of Northwest seashore developments—a metropolis magnificent as it spread across drawing board and newspaper advertisement but strictly one-horse in its actuality on the beach. Pacific City did have one interesting distinction, however, a San Francisco hotel, which the town's creator, Dr. Elijah White, had purchased fully equipped in San Francisco for $28,000 and shipped north on the *Carolina* for reassembly.

The first man to see the possibilities in what became the townsite of Portland was Captain John H. Couch, a New England sea peddler, who came up the Columbia in 1840, pausing along the way to sell from the decks of his vessel various items of merchandise supplied by the Cushings of Newburyport, Massachusetts. Of the alder-forested plain where the Willamette meets the Columbia, near the spot where the Indians had cleaned about an acre of land in gathering wood for their camp fires, Captain Couch said, "To this point I can bring any ship that can get into the mouth of the Great Columbia River." It was a remark that fits admirably the pattern of understatement preferred by Portlanders, and there is also perhaps something symbolic in the fact that Captain Couch waited five years before going into business himself at Portland.

The first white man actually to settle within the present boundaries of Portland was a French-Canadian employee of the Hudson's Bay Company, who came in 1829 but soon went away. Next an Englishman, William Johnson, built a cabin in what is now South Portland and went into manufacturing, his product being a drink known to history as "blue ruin," but Johnson died. In 1843, William Overton of Tennessee, by way of Oregon City, stopped at the Indian camp ground while on a canoe trip and decided to claim it. Lacking money for a formal survey, or even for filing a claim, Overton offered a half-interest in the square-mile site to Asa Lawrence Lovejoy of Groton, Massachusetts, in recompense for financing the claim. Lovejoy agreed. Overton, however, quickly tired of pioneering and, after selling his remaining half of the claim to Francis W. Pettygrove for fifty dollars, departed for Texas where, according to legend, he was hanged. The new owners, Lovejoy and Pettygrove, could not agree whether to name their townsite after the largest city of Lovejoy's native Massachusetts or of Pettygrove's native Maine. They decided to flip a coin to determine the matter but with New England conservatism declined to risk all on a single toss. The penny, in three spins, landed once heads for Boston, twice tails for Portland.

Pettygrove built a log store at what developed into Front and Washington streets and started a wagon road back into the hills. When Lieutenants Warre and Vavavour of the British Army, traveling incognito through the Northwest to gather information that might be useful to the Crown in deciding the boundary controversy, reached the clearing on the Willamette they found a hamlet that "had only then received a name and its inhabitants were felling the trees from which their first homes were to be constructed and their primitive furniture was to be made. With such tools only as saw, auger, pole-ax, broad-ax and adze, those men labored with zeal that atoned for want of better implements."

The pioneer shortage of machine tools was not confined to carpentry. When John Waymire, a Missourian, built Portland's first mill, the industry was wryly described as "a whipsaw, two men, and a log."

Neither Lovejoy nor Pettygrove stuck it out at Portland. The former sold his share of the townsite to Benjamin Stark, and Pettygrove earned the city's eternal gratitude by swapping the other half to Daniel H. Lownsdale for five thousand dollars worth of leather and hides—not much for half a city, perhaps, but a hundred times more than he had paid for it four years earlier.

Kentucky-born and widely traveled, Lownsdale knew a good thing when he saw it, and had not only an instinct for promotion but financial resources and able friends. He interested Stephen Coffin, a Maine promoter then resident at Oregon City, and William W. Chapman, a Virginia attorney who had sailed west with the first Forty-Niners, in helping him develop Portland. Together they organized the Portland Townsite Company. Coffin also went into the transportation business, establishing a canoe ferry and freight service. By 1848 a diarist could boast that "Portland has two white houses and one brick, and three wood-colored frame houses and a few cabins."

There were several such settlements with a chance at dominance. The touchstone for town promotion in that time and place was embedded less in industrial development than in transportation. Those towns prospered that touched deep water and drained farmland. The Inland Empire beyond the Cascades remained, then, the province of the Indian and the trapper; the productive farmlands were concentrated along the valleys of the Willamette and its eastward-flowing tributary, the Tulatin. The question of the day was: which community will succeed in getting the necessary docks built, the roads laid, the shipping lines established, and the hotels erected to trap the transient dollar?

Oregon City had the head start. Oregon City was rooted on the benchlands where the Willamette, flowing northward between the Coastal Mountains and the Cascades, parallel to the Pacific, breaks downward over a forty-foot basalt ledge. At this point the Hudson's Bay Company, having belatedly decided that the fur country south of the river could no longer be kept empty of white occupants and that it would be more advisable to encourage settlement by those favorable to the Crown than to permit the unchallenged westward migration of Americans, permitted Factor John McLoughlin, that wild-haired, steel-eyed executive, to "set up a sawmill at the falls of the Wilhamet . . . where the same Establishment of people [might] attend to the mill, watch the Fur & Salmon trade, and take care of a Stock of Cattle."

The Company settlement, planted (along with potatoes) in the spring of 1829, attracted during its first decade not only partisans of the Crown but sufficient Americans to support a Temperance Society whose pitch was that liquor in log cabins incited not only intemperance among the white inhabitants but the unwanted and energetic attentions of the aborigines. By 1843, while William Johnson was still brewing blue ruin in the fastness of South Portland, Oregon City was large enough to support the Oregon Lyceum and the Falls Debating Society, which were arguing such topics as "Resolved, That it is expedient for settlers on this coast to establish an independent government." Appropriately, Oregon City became the first provisional and territorial capital of Oregon and the first town to be incorporated under American law west of the Missouri. As depot for the freight coming from the upper reaches of the Willamette, and despite the handicap of rapids between it and the Columbia, the town at the falls was a serious competitor for regional dominance. Also in the running were Milwaukie, a few miles downstream. Milwaukie had a working sawmill; the energetic sponsorship of Lot Whitcomb, a man untroubled by doubts or modesty; and the advantage of being below the Clackamas rapids, where the river "wore through at the bottom" in low water. A bit farther down was Linnton, speculative effort by Peter Burnett and Morton McCarver, who was later to found Tacoma. Linnton failed rapidly, according to its promoters because Oregon City merchants maintained a near corner on house nails.

The struggle for supremacy on the Willamette, and eventually the Columbia, diminished from a free-for-all among several contenders to a duel between Oregon City and Portland. The town at the falls had the advantage that all shipments from the most productive farm area in the territory had to be unloaded and reloaded there; Portland had the advantage that the Clackamas rapids made it difficult for boats to run between Oregon City and the Columbia. The river could be navigated, however: numerous keel boats, bateaux, and canoes made it, and so did a man named Truesdale, who made a successful run from Portland to Oregon City with a craft eighty-two feet long, propelled by paddles driven by six horses on a treadmill. The fact that the contraption worked only made people along the river more than ever optimistic about steamers.

The first commercial steamer to reach the Columbia on a regular run was the Pacific Mail Company's *Carolina,* which came in May 1850, inaugurating what was supposed to be a monthly mail run from California. The company first announced Astoria as its terminus, and later—to Portland's dismay—moved its docks to St. Helens, where the town promoters talked of running a shortline railroad over the mountains to siphon off the cargoes of the Tulatin plains.

The *Carolina* was followed by the smaller, independently owned sidewheeler, the *Gold Hunter,* which arrived in search of both cargo and financial backing. Portlanders, realizing the advantages of a steamer of their own, pungled up some $60,000 for what they believed to be a decisive interest in the paddle-wheeler and happily announced Portland as northern terminus of the coastal run. But when the *Gold Hunter* got back to San Francisco, her former operators (perhaps with financial aid from Pacific Mail) bought the stock held by the ship's officers, regained control of her destiny, and sent her off to service on the Mexican Coast.

Meanwhile, handymen at both Astoria and Milwaukie were going into the steamboat business on a do-it-yourself basis. The Astoria vessel was a double-ended sidewheeler of low power and no grace, described by a passenger as "not at all a harbor of comfort" but capable of making two runs a month between Astoria and Oregon City. Called the *Columbia,* she did not long have her namesake to herself. On Christmas day, 1850, there was launched at Milwaukie by the town proprietor, Lot Whitcomb, a sturdier and more powerful river boat, called the *Lot Whitcomb of Oregon,* which took to the water accompanied by a speech by Whitcomb, delivered in what was described as his "usual and happy style" by the *Western Star,* Lot Whitcomb's newspaper.

Portland, Oregon, and Mount Hood in the moonlight.

Tacoma's Narrows Bridge, "Sturdy Gertie," is the successor to "Galloping Gertie," which fell into Puget Sound on November 7, 1940.

Seattle's Floating Bridge, across Lake Washington, rides on great concrete pontoons. Puget Sound and the Olympics lie beyond.

Vancouver, British Columbia, at night, seen from Grouse Mountain.

ew of the Olympic Mountains from a Seattle restaurant.

123

A Portland bridge rises out of the morning mist that steams from the Willamette River, while in the distance Mount Hood serenely reaches into the high overcast.

During the autumn and winter months, rain is a way of life west of the Cascades.

The Port of Tacoma has been built on tide-flats reclaimed by diking and filling. The industrial area is one of the major complexes of the electro-chemical industry in the West, but, as the clustered rafts show, Tacoma still saws, pulps, and remolds much lumber.

OPPOSITE: *Our cities are seaports. The freighter is passing West Point Light, outward bound from Seattle.*

Portraits on the Seattle waterfront.

OS: JOSEF SCAYLEA

Seattle's Olde Curiosity Shop, where tourists can find anything from almost authentic shrunken heads to an Indian rain hat.

Skid Road Mission in Seattle.

On a warm summer evening the pattern of lights and men tells the story of life along the Skid Road in the lower Burnside section of Portland.

The Seattle Art Museum in Volunteer Park.

Thunderbird Park in Victoria, British Columbia, where the finest handicrafts of British Columbia Indian totem pole carvers are exhibited.

Figurehead from the Empress of Japan, *in Stanley Park, Vancouver, British Columbia.*

The Astoria (Oregon) Column, depicting the history of the Old Oregon country.

The historic Forestry Building, which was constructed for the Lewis and Clark Exposition in 1903, is the largest log structure in the world. It is now a museum of forest products and one of the principal sight-seeing attractions in Portland.

RAY ATKESON

131

Inside the city limits of Seattle.

JOSEF SCAYLEA

*The nearness of the sea can make
even the garbage dump look lovely.*

Bears in Woodland Park in Seattle.

133

At the International Rose Test Gardens of Washington Park in Portland, there are several acres of carefully tended roses, and new varieties from all over the world are grown by experts who keep accurate records of the characteristics of each rose.

This tulip farm lies in the Puyallup Valley, ten minu. from downtown Tacoma.

Residents of Portland can look out across forested valleys to snow-capped mountains. This is a view of the Willamette River valley.

At the edge of the big cities lie the lovely farms. Happy Valley, as the residents call this area on the southeast outskirts of Portland, is a mile long and two miles wide. About a dozen farmers still live here, although subdivision has begun.

Whitcomb had reason for his immodesty. The *Lot Whitcomb* was a fine boat, and her captain, J. C. Ainsworth, an exceptionally able man. An orphan at seven, Ainsworth had become a Mississippi River pilot in his teens and master of a vessel in his early twenties; as skipper he taught many other men the tricks of the upper river, and years later he was presented with a massive gold watch by a grateful former pilot, Samuel Clemens. Ainsworth had come west during the gold rush with William C. Ralston, who later organized the Bank of California. In spite of his merits, Captain Ainsworth on his second cruise down the Willamette managed to hang the *Lot Whitcomb* on a reef opposite the Clackamas River, from which, to the unconcealed delight of Portlanders, it took a fortnight to free her. The *Lot Whitcomb* survived the grounding and, until her sale to California interests in 1854, rated as queen of the river.

In 1851 the Pacific Mail Company gave up on St. Helens and decided on Portland as its northern terminus, which all but settled the question of which city would dominate shipping on the Willamette and lower Columbia. The growth of California as the result of the Gold Rush had increased demand for food, lumber, and leather from the Northwest. This in turn led to a shipping boom on the lower Columbia, while the Indian wars led to the development of upstream transportation. From all this, Portland business interests benefited, none more so than Captain Ainsworth.

In the first decade of commercial steam operations on the Columbia, the captain and his associate Simeon G. Reed, a wholesale liquor and grocery dealer, gained control of most of the shipping west of the Cascades. Above the rapids an ex-Indian agent from Ohio, R. R. Thompson, had a near monopoly, while at the Cascades the Bradford brothers transshipped cargoes six miles on a horse-drawn railroad, and, at the second portage above the Dalles, Orlando Humason and J. S. Ruckle loaded the goods onto horsecarts. Thus all freight moving between the Inland Empire and Portland was carried on three boats, a one-horse railroad, and a horsecart, each adding a separate charge.

The idea of consolidating the services into a single monopoly must have occurred to many. Captain Ainsworth was the one who pulled it off. First he arranged a loose alliance, the Union Transportation Line, which embraced the rival steamboat interests but did not take in the portage people. When that lash-up proved ineffectual, Ainsworth incorporated (with Reed and Thompson his chief associates) the air-tight Oregon Steam Navigation Company, known affectionately as the O.S.N., and not so affectionately as the Monopoly. The O.S.N.'s reputation for charging all the traffic would bear was such that when housewives complained at paying two bits for a single needle, storekeepers replied, "But we have to add the freight."

Glenn Chesney Quiett, in his robust history of western transportation, *They*

Built the West (New York: Appleton-Century, 1934), tells of the Monopoly's ingenious method of simplifying freight charges:

> Forty cubic feet was assumed to be a ton, no matter what the actual weight might be. To calculate the weight of a wagon, its length was measured from the rear wheel to the end of the tongue; then the tongue was turned up at right angles, and the height was measured from wheel-base to tip of tongue. These dimensions served to determine the freight-charges; no scales were needed; and after the measurements were made, the tongue was detached and put under the wagon bed to save space.

Under this system articles weighing as little as two hundred pounds might measure a ton, and at the rate of forty dollars for each forty cubic feet from Portland to Lewis a shipper might be paying as much as a dollar a mile. A legend persists that, confronted with the problem of how to measure a cannon, which was so compact and so heavy that it did not look profitable on the cubic-foot basis, a well-trained agent of the Monopoly thoughtfully hitched a mule to it and measured them together.

The O.S.N. effectively blocked the growth of small, independent lines that might develop into serious competition. It refused to handle cargo hauled by anyone else in its area unless the shipper paid the Monopoly its regular rate for every mile the competitor had moved the goods. On the other hand, no matter how raw the Monopoly's use of economic force against the rivals and with the customers at its mercy, O.S.N. maintained fast and comfortable service on a tight schedule; under the dictatorship, the boats ran on time.

Just after Oregon Steam Navigation closed its grip on the river system, gold was discovered in the eastern reaches of Washington Territory (now Idaho). The lure of the placer mines drew men and machines up the river. Some who came to prospect stayed to farm. The Indians were further circumscribed. Towns were born. On the trade with this emergent country the O.S.N. and Portland battened.

Meanwhile, up on Puget Sound, rival ports were developing. The first towns on the shore of the sea in the forest did not have to worry about the considerable dangers and even worse reputation of the Columbia bar; but they were at the great disadvantage of having nothing to sell. Some wheat was grown on the Nisqually plains; a few bolts of cedar were cut; a few head of bleating cattle were sometimes swung by their long horns down into the holds of ships bound for Russian America: but there was no single product that drew ships—not until the California Gold Rush. The same "population explosion" in California that had provided a market for the produce of the Willamette valley made cutting down trees along the Sound profitable. San Francisco required piling and plank for its docks, more shakes for its roofs, more boards and battens for its walls, more ties for its railroads than the existing hamlets on the Sound were able to supply.

So it was that when Captain Daniel Howard of the brig *Leonesa,* en route to Olympia from San Francisco in December 1851, noticed a scattering of new cabins on the southwesterly point of land guarding Elliott Bay, he hove to and inquired of the settlers if they had pilings for sale. They did not. The little group of transplanted Midwesterners had been at Alki Point only a few weeks and their time had been taken up trying to get roofs on their cabins. But cash was cash, and cutting down trees as a way to make a quick buck seemed more certain than waiting for property values to rise. They told Captain Howard that when the *Leonesa* got back from Olympia they'd have lumber for him to load; and they did, though the loading proved difficult in the shallow waters off the point. Right there the majority of the pioneers learned an important lesson: if you want a waterfront town to prosper, and you with it, the town needs good anchorage.

For the next few weeks three men from the pioneer colony—Arthur Denny, William Bell, and Carson Boren—spent much of their time in a small boat, engaged in that familiar Puget Sound pastime of looking for desirable waterfront property. The hunt was not without risks. None of the three was an experienced boatsman; all were suffering from ague, a malaria-like complaint marked by alternate chills and fever. At best an Indian dugout is tricky and the shifting winds of winter can seem malevolent. Yet they persisted.

First they coasted the shoreline south of Alki, checking possible sites at Three Tree Point, Redondo, and Dash Point; they may have passed Brown's Point to look into Commencement Bay, where later Tacoma grew, but they did not find what they were seeking—low bank fronting deep water with conifers convenient to the shore and enough open land nearby to support the livestock they had left wintering down on the Willamette.

Early in February 1852 the three men set out across Elliott Bay to explore the far shore. They took with them a clothesline and horseshoes for sounding water depth. They left about dawn and those who came to the beach were worried. "Don't lose the horseshoes," one of the men called after them. Mary Denny, who had a four-month-old to wash for, warned her husband to take care of the clothesline.

They crossed to what is now called Smith's Cove and began taking soundings. Bell and Boren handled the dugout while Denny heaved the horseshoes. The water proved delightfully deep but the clay bank was too high and the beach too narrow. They worked back around the shore toward Alki. While lunching on the beach, Denny noticed a break in the trees. He climbed the bank and found a clearing that apparently had been made by fire; rejoining Boren and Bell he said he thought he would claim the land.

By mid-afternoon the party came to an area of low bank across which a small stream wandered. Beyond the stream the forest rose again, and at the edge of the forest stood the poles of an Indian summer house. This was what the settlers wanted in the way of land; but was the water deep? Denny heaved the horseshoes and the line ran out and out. The exploring party returned across the bay to tell their people that they had found what they sought. A few days later, February 15, they paddled back and without ceremony drove the stakes for their claims in what is now downtown Seattle. Since Alki did not officially become a part of Seattle for nearly sixty years, this was the real birthday of the city.

Succeeding birthdays were well celebrated, for Seattle had a damp childhood in ways other than climatic. When Charles Terry had landed at Alki Point along with the other founding fathers, he came prepared to do a little trading. With him were a box of tinware, a box of axes, a box of raisins, a keg of brandy, and a keg of whisky. Another member of the party recalled long afterward that prior to the coming of the whites "Alki had not been a general camping place for the Indians but soon after we landed . . . they commenced to congregate, and continued coming until we had over a thousand there, and most of them remained all winter." The magnet that drew the stolid Salish to the new town may have been tin pans or raisins rather than alcohol, but certainly something happened to the contents of young Terry's kegs. When the brig *Leonesa* sailed back to San Francisco with pilings the settlers had cut, Terry sent down an order for more whisky.

Seattle's reputation as a good place to visit was heightened the following spring with the arrival from Olympia of David Swinson Maynard, who besides being a certified practitioner of the medical arts was a Jack of all trades and a master of elbow bending. Doc Maynard had been running a small store in Olympia, where he made himself the hero of his customers and the despair of competitors by cutting prices with each drink. The doctor was a hard-drinking man; as his turnover increased his profit decreased. After Chief Sealth, tyee of the Duwamish tribe, met Maynard on a visit up sound and suggested there were plenty of customers available in the neighborhood of the Duwamish, the good doctor loaded his goods on a scow and went north.

Maynard arrived just as the first settlers were moving across the bay from Alki. They obligingly adjusted boundaries to accommodate him with waterfront property. He raised a store eighteen feet wide by twenty-six feet long, with log walls and a shake roof—the Seattle Exchange. (It was Maynard who suggested the village be named after his Indian friend Sealth.) Maynard's place became the center of entertainment and political action in early Seattle, and Maynard the town's most persistent though least prosperous booster.

Maynard's Seattle Exchange eventually gave way to Yesler's cook-house as social center. The log cookhouse was ancillary to Yesler's steam mill, the root of Seattle's early success; it was the first steam mill on the sound. Henry Yesler, a native of Maryland and like many another early lumberman a fellow of little education but focused energy, had learned about sawmilling in Ohio, accumulated some capital, and decided to go to California to play for bigger stakes. Not liking the prospects around San Francisco, he came north looking over sites in the Douglas fir country. Seattle seemed promising, but the only good location for a mill was on property already claimed by Maynard and Boren. In the best tradition of town promoters they moved their claims to make room for a man with a payroll.

Yesler's mill did more than give the town its first permanent payroll. Commercial establishments offering clothing and food by day and other creature comforts by night sprang up, thus enriching not only the entrepreneurs but the language. The rumored delights along the skid road lured visitors and dollars to the little town.

But Seattle's monopoly on steam and sin was soon broken. More mills were built on other bays and coves, and Seattle's industrial head start was not enough to assure its long-run supremacy. The secret of success, everyone felt, lay in transportation. Inevitably a railroad would reach across the continent to the Pacific Northwest, and the town that became the terminus would have greatness conferred upon it and wealth upon its citizens. It mattered not that Portlanders considered the question of a northwest terminus settled; on Puget Sound it was an article of faith that terminating rails on a river with a tricky channel and a fatal bar, when there was available unobstructed salt water, would indeed be a hell of a way to run a railroad.

On all the sound there breathed no town with soul so dead that it did not think it would be chosen. Towns perched on high clay banks, towns settled drearily beside swamps, towns unbuilt, towns on islands all waited in blissful anticipation of the Day One Would Be Chosen.

When the great day came, in July 1873, and the Northern Pacific announced its choice, the winner was not bustling Seattle; not old Olympia with its territorial capital and its guardian mud flats; not Steilacoom with its celebrated night life and its pretensions to culture; not Mukilteo, or Nisqually, or Port Townsend, but an all but non-existent hamlet at the head of Commencement Bay called Tacoma.

As a native Tacoman, I feel that the Northern Pacific's choice can be defended on the grounds of economics and geography; but the feeling of rival communities was less sympathetic. They decried the selection of Tacoma as madness or worse; they were quick to note that Northern Pacific officials had formed the Tacoma Land Company to dispose of tracts in the terminal city as property values rose. They appealed vainly to Congress to declare forfeit the land grant which the federal government had allocated the Northern Pacific to underwrite construction costs. They made the traditional gestures of starting their own railroads to be built with the sweat of the citizens' brows; Seattle's line actually got as far as the coalfields in the hills behind Renton.

From Tacoma's point of view, the trouble with the Northern Pacific as fairy godfather was that the railroad was a schizophrenic with a penchant for bankruptcy, the occupational disease of transcontinental railroads. The brains of the N.P. were divided about the desirability of Tacoma as a terminus. Charles B. Wright, who from time to time served as president of the Northern Pacific and most of the time was president of the Tacoma Land Company, was Tacoma's most determined advocate. The town's most dangerous foe, within company ranks, was Henry Villard, the Bavarian-born scholar turned financier, who twice controlled the board. Villard had acquired the Oregon Steam Navigation company in a fantastic piece of financial sleight-of-hand and had used the O.S.N. in his maneuvers to get possession of the N.P.; under the circumstances, he favored Portland as terminus for, as Wright would benefit by anything that helped Tacoma and its land company, Villard would benefit by all the encouraged growth of Portland and Columbia river traffic. Villard had a second string on his financial bow. He had quietly purchased the old Seattle citizen-started line to the coalfields. If a Puget Sound port was to win terminal status, Villard favored Seattle.

While Wright and his friends had the say, track was pushed north from Kalama on the Columbia to Tacoma. Whenever Villard was on top, efforts were concentrated on pushing the line down the south bank of the Columbia and on improving Portland's terminal facilities and wharfage. During the N.P.'s periodic spasms of bankruptcy, when work stopped, Portland clamored for government dredging and jetty-building on the Columbia; Tacoma argued the urgency of bypassing Portland and its troublesome river by constructing the main line from Eastern Washington over the Cascades to Puget Sound, preferably by way of Naches Pass, the break in the range nearest Tacoma.

The Northern Pacific board, under the threat of Congressional forfeiture of its land grant in the Cascades, in 1886 ordered construction of the Cascade Division line. Although the route chosen was through Stampede Pass, which emerged disturbingly close to Seattle, the announcement of the decision touched off wild speculation in Tacoma property. Rudyard Kipling, visiting the town, claimed a Tacoman nearly pulled a gun on a friend who didn't agree that the City of Destiny (as George Francis Train, the eastern eccentric, had dubbed Tacoma) would outstrip San Francisco without working up a sweat. The ultimate collapse of this boom left physical and mental trauma still discernible in Tacoma.

Seattle had by no means given up hope of winning a railroad—any railroad, Tacoma's or some other. Let down by Villard, the inhabitants next pinned their hopes on James Jerome Hill, the one-eyed, grizzle-bearded genius at empire-building, who was driving the Great Northern west. Hill came through, bringing his line first over the Marias Pass into the inter-mountain country, then over the Snoqualmie Pass and down the western slope of the Cascades to Seattle.

Though the Great Northern arrived with the depression, its presence proved decisive. In self-defense the Northern Pacific had to replace its bobtail line from Tacoma—which had run on a schedule calculated to force Seattleites to sit out long periods in their rival community—with regular service. Hill arranged for ships of the Nippon Yusen Kaisha, Japan's great steamship line, to call at Seattle, which stimulated other waterfront development. So it was that when gold was discovered in the Klondike Seattle had the facilities to serve as a major port of embarkation.

It was Seattle's great fortune that in the town at the time of the Klondike excitement was Erastus Brainerd, former curator of engravings at the Boston Art Museum, who had taken a turn at journalism and was about to prove himself a genius at publicity. Asked by Seattle business interests to publicize the city as the gateway to gold, Brainerd selected his keynotes with delicate precision, then used every device known to medicine man or the pre-Madison Avenue practitioners of persuasion to augment them. Brainerd's success was stunning. Of the adventurers who sailed north to seek the gold in pockets in the ground or the gold in other men's pockets, more sailed from and returned to Seattle than went through all the other ports combined. They went as tenderfoot cheechakos, they came back as veteran sourdoughs, and going and coming they left money in Seattle.

With the largesse of the gold rush, Seattle had capital to lower the hills that impeded its growth, fill in its tidelands, connect its lakes by canals, and lay the foundation for the shipbuilding industry which, in turn, helped create the aircraft industry that today gives employment to sixty thousand persons.

The growth of Seattle at a site unsupported by river communication and not particularly favored by geology remains a topic for debate among economists: is Seattle in the logical location for the metropolis, or was its development a matter of spirit triumphing over geography? There are no such arguments about Vancouver. The great city of western Canada was certain to rise where the rails reached water, and the only logical path for track through the mountains was down the valley of the Fraser. The question was not where, but when. Having joined the other provinces to form Canada on the promise of being provided a rail connection with the East, British Columbia for years shook the needles from the hemlock with bellows of protest at each delay in completion. In 1886 the Canadian Pacific came down the Fraser through Hell's Gate and reached salt water. A metropolis at the point was assured.

Just twenty years earlier, Captain Edward Stamp had built a sawmill inside what is now Vancouver, a cranky steam mill which meant there would be a village. The captain was a dour chap with mutton-chop whiskers, a man solidly built but not solid financially. He went broke and in 1870 the Hastings Sawmill Company acquired the mill and its adjacent store. The store still stands, a museum now, and among its framed documents is a charming account by an early storekeeper of the early operations; from the facts given by Salvert Simpson it is easy to project a picture of the life of the remote logging village:

We carried a general line of groceries, tobacco, cigars, pipes, men's suits (at first brought out from England, with pants so high-cut one hardly needed a vest), overalls, underwear made of flannel all wool branded Mission, in blue and red color, the red in big demand as a supposed cure for rheumatism, these were made in Victoria; also a fleecy underwear with a nap, shirts, socks and a line of men's rough work shoes, both laces and elastic sides, made in Victoria. . . .

A line of patent medicine was carried, such as Thomas Electric Oil, Pain Killer, Peruna, Pains Celery Compound—the two latter being 75 per cent alcohol were in much demand in the camps after a big drunk. Jamaica Ginger was not allowed to be sold to Indians as government claimed they used it to make liquor. St. Jacobs Oil, Wizard Oil, Scented Hair Oil, Red Rouge for Indian face colouring, Ammonia 880 Linaments, Cough mixtures and other patents too numerous to mention.

A line of tinware [was] bought from a New Westminster tin smith. English white unbreakable crockery for camp use. A line of hardware such as rope, axes, single and double bit, saws, nails, files, axe handles, locks, hinges, etc., oxbows, ox shoes, hickory goad sticks for the bull puncher, who was very particular as to quality. The bull puncher or teamster usually drove twelve oxen and was the highest paid man in camp. A yoke of two oxen in 1871 cost $200.

Matches were the smelly sulphur kind put in blocks in five gallon coal oil tins. Matches were made in Victoria. Canned Sockeye Salmon put up in one-pound tall tins, the bellies salted were sold in kits (½ barrels and barrels) only the bellies were used, the other parts were thrown away. No other species of salmon was canned. A lot of Corned Beef and Pork in barrels was sent to the Logging Camps, also green salt sides of Bacon to make Pork and Beans. Fresh Meat was sent to the camps only when a tug went after a boom of logs. Fresh ham and eggs were only supplied at Easter. No fresh fruit was used. Rhubarb in season, dried apples and prunes were the standbys. Dried apple pie went by the name of Stick Pie in the camps. . . . In Granville fresh eggs at Christmas were often $1.00 a dozen. A sloop used to come over from the Sound with eggs and green apples and go back with a load of lumber. Ham was dearer than bacon and much fatter. They had not begun to raise the long lean bacon as now. Venison was plentiful in season with no restrictions as to sale, also wild ducks. A man named Wragg used to sell venison as low as five cents a pound. The Indians used to shoot the deer for the hide, leaving the carcass to rot. I used to, as Agent for Jack Green, a trader, who was murdered later on Savory Island, sell dried deer skins to a buyer named Marcus Baldy for 28¢ a pound, who exported to the United States, where they were tanned and made into lace leather for belting.

Thus, Vancouver on the eve of rails. Victoria, at the time was the major city of western Canada, having been selected in 1842 by James Douglas of the Hudson's Bay Company as the site for a fort, because the fields behind the harbor could provide ample food for the garrison. Douglas described the area at the southern tip of Vancouver Island as "the most picturesque and decidedly most valuable Part of the Island that we had the good Fortune to discover." Bruce Hutchison, the Canadian writer, a native of Victoria, has called it "a sweep of barren rock, a ravine of stinking tidal mud, and the cedar huts of an Indian village."

Douglas, in choosing the site for Victoria, had not planned on establishing a city. He was simply interested in adequate headquarters for Hudson's Bay Company agricultural and fur operations in the West, beyond the likely reach of American expansion. And for more than a decade Victoria developed as Douglas had expected, becoming a community of pipe-smoking Britishers who worked the rich soil (gardening is still a quiet passion and a way of life for most Victorians) while their cattle fattened and the company boats stopped in from time to time with the accumulations of pelts from the outposts. Douglas could take quiet pride in the fact that in the country retained by the Crown after the settlement with the United States a way of life was developing which, while profitable, was unlikely to attract an influx of Yankees.

Then in 1858 news of the discovery of gold on the Fraser reached the outside world, and everything changed. Though the strike had been a hundred miles up the Fraser and Victoria was on the island at some distance removed from even the mouth of the river, it was the only British port with adequate supplies on the way to the gold fields; besides, official permission was required to transport anyone up the Fraser, and Victoria was the place to ask it. Men by the thousands rushed to the quiet island village to outfit themselves; others came to supply their wants. The price of lots in Victoria and neighboring Esquimalt rose from five to five hundred dollars or more as, within months, twenty thousand persons camped around the town and ten thousand more crossed the strait and started up the Fraser.

Commander Richard Charles Mayne of H. M. Survey Vessel *Plumper* had been in Victoria just before the rush and returned to find the pleasant village buried under a human deluge, and the very character of the earlier inhabitants transformed. "Everyone whom a few weeks ago we had left engaged steadily in pursuits from which they were reaping a slow, sure profit seemed to have gone gold mad," he noted. "That road . . . from Esquimalt to Victoria . . . was changed almost beyond recognition. Only a few months before, we used to flounder through the mud without meeting a single soul; now it was covered with pedestrians toiling along, with the step and air of men whose minds are occupied with thoughts of business; crowded with well-laden carts and vans, with Wells Fargo's, or Freeman's 'expresses,' and with strangers of every tongue and country, in every variety of attire."

The Fraser, too, swarmed with men. They fought their way upstream toward the gold-spangled bars, some in canoes, others feeling their way along the dangerous trails which had been little improved since Simon Fraser's day. Before the Fraser rush, and the subsequent excitement in the Cariboo, farther to the east, petered out, roads were developed, towns flowered only to wither, and the legend that the Fraser valley was unsuitable for cultivation was laid to rest. The influx of prospectors, some of whom settled in the country, led to the decline in the relative importance of the Hudson's Bay Company; with the expiration of its charter, H.B.C. became not the chosen instrument for operating much of the area but merely another private citizen, albeit one of considerable influence. The decline of the Company's status was furthered by the rise of the sawmill industry, which infringed on areas previously considered suitable only for the production of furs.

Such then was the situation when the Canadian Pacific Railway thrust rails across the continent. British Columbia Indians have many myths about Demigods Who Changed Things; their pantheon might well include the C.P.R.

The arrival of the railroad stimulated industrial development and concentrated it at the mouth of the Fraser. The little hamlets already in existence coalesced into the town called Vancouver. Fed by lumber from the coastal range, by wheat from the central plains ("People had to adjust to using more water for hard wheat flour than for American soft," an old-timer recalls, "and besides, the Indians who used the empty sacks for underwear complained that the jute sack of Manitoba was not so comfortable next to the skin as the cotton American sack"), by apples from the Okanogan, by salmon and halibut from the rivers and the ocean (to which were added later pulp from Powell River, copper from the smelter at Trail, aluminum from the potlines at Kitimat), Vancouver grew from town to city to metropolis. Today the ships of the world (Canadian policy has not cut Vancouver off from trade with the Chinese mainland) nuzzle up to the docks beneath the solid skyline that rises in the shadow of the mountains.

Though the boom has tapered off, Vancouver is still growing more rapidly than either Portland or Seattle. Opinions are mixed as to whether this expansion is to be applauded. Bruce Hutchison, the Victorian, feels that Vancouver's best days (the days when the scent of cedar was sharp in the air, and the city's roots were in the forest) are behind her; he describes the city as "this distillate of jungle and ocean, this mixture of beauty and ugliness, this ever spreading fungus of wealth and slums, this woodland clearing where man has heaped up overnight the brassiest, loveliest, craziest of all Canadian towns, and now worships his inferior masterpiece in childlike wonder, fierce greed, and a sure conviction of superiority."

An English journalist of my acquaintance, who has seen an extraordinary number of the world's great cities, tells me he can think of none with a superior setting, but adds, "nor is there any city that reminds me more of Los Angeles, which, among places to live, I consider the nadir." Mort Sahl on a visit to Vancouver in 1961 likened it to East Berlin. The letter columns of the Vancouver papers are studded with brutal comment about the aesthetic judgments of those in charge, while front-page headlines in Second Coming type proclaim narcotics rings, burglary rings, bungling, and corruption. Yet even this criticism and carping seems more a demonstration of the city's vitality than an indictment; a visitor from Seattle or Portland may find it smacks nostalgically of the fierce feuds and bitter judgments that marked an earlier era in his own town. Not that Portland or Seattle find themselves shy of internal critics: Vancouver's animadverters simply seem more enthusiastic.

Each of the great cities of the Northwest merits the censure of those who cite the violation often done to the splendor of the surroundings. In none of them do men's additions consistently embellish nature to the degree they might. But each city remains, to most of its citizens, a great place to live in. Residents of Seattle, Portland, and Vancouver envy their friends who go on trips, but we feel sorry for those who must move away.

PLAYGROUND

A POET HAS said, "Seattle has a love affair with water," and a banker has pointed out that the writer understated the situation: the passion is shared by the entire Northwest.

The rains water the forests and feed the rivers that support the basic industries of the region. Water makes the Northwest wheels go round. But it is during their leisure hours that the people of the area become most passionately involved with water: fresh or salt, flowing or impounded, as snowfield or glacier, stream or lake or ocean, we of the Northwest seek water to ride on, splash in, swim under, fish, shoot over, or simply stare at. We are aquaphiles, congenital and content.

More people own boats in the Puget Sound area than anywhere in the country; there are more power boats per capita than anywhere else in the world. Nearly anyone can afford a boat, and it costs less to belong to most yacht clubs in the Northwest than to golf clubs or even fraternal organizations.

In an area of unsurpassed natural beauty, living as they do in towns girded by salt water or traversed by navigable rivers—towns which may also enfold

ATKESON

The Northwest Corner is a paradise for travelers who love scenic beauty. One of the most famous spots is Crater Lake, Oregon, the lake an incredibly blue lagoon in the crater of an extinct volcano. This view is from a plane flying at 13,000 feet.

149

Rowboats and rubber rafts run the white waters of the McKenzie River in Oregon at the opening of the fishing season.

RAY ATKESON

The University of Washington's racing shells, followed by the coach's launch, skim through the Montlake Cut, which connects Lake Washington with Lake Union, in Seattle.

JOSEF SCAYLEA

JOSEF SCAYLEA

ABOVE: *In the early days on Puget Sound, tugs raced from the Sound ports to the entrance of the Strait of Juan de Fuca whenever the Tatoosh station telegraphed that a sailing ship was in sight. The winner was awarded the right to tow the craft to mill or grain elevator. Now boats from Seattle, Tacoma, Vancouver, and other ports spend most of their time pulling log booms or barges. But every year or so, there is a tugboat race for the Broom, symbolic of sweeping the Sound.*

FORDE PHOTOGRAPHERS

ABOVE: *Crowds estimated by Seattle police at a quarter of a million jam the shores of Lake Washington to watch the Gold Cup, a hydroplane race, one of the features of Seattle's Sea Fair each August.*

Fold-boating. Here a kayaker runs the rapids on Green River in western Washington.

151

JOSEF SCAYLEA

There are more boats per capita in the Puget Sound area than anywhere else in the world. On a sunny day one sees many an impromptu ballet of sail.

Clam-digging beside a derelict of the sea buried in the sands at Long Beach, Washington.

RAY ATKESON

JOSEF SCAYLEA

OPPOSITE: *A troop of Boy Scouts try seat-of-the-pants skiing in Rainier National Park.*

"There is," oldtimers assure the gullible, "no sport quite like hunting geoducks from horseback." At the left, Haystack Rock, Cannon Beach, Oregon.

AL MONNER

Trout-fishing on the Metolius River in Oregon.

RAY ATKESON

When the smelt start running, every man and his son dip smelt from the Sandy in Oregon near its confluence with the Columbia.

A skier at timberline on Mount Baker near Bellingham, Washington.

BELOW: *Mountaineers working their way across Toutle Glacier on Mount St. Helens, Washington.*

lakes—most Northwesterners accept water as a way of life. Many a working man whose house overlooks ocean, strait or sound, river or lake, still feels the need to get away from it all and maintains a summer place—a "shack" if on the beach, a "cabin" if in the mountains, though the words may describe houses complete with running water, electricity, television, and sometimes a swimming pool. A Tacoma friend of mine (not rich) has his town house on a suburban stream ten minutes from his office, a beach place on Puget Sound, a mountain place on a lake.

Water, water everywhere, and all of it alluring. I happen to live by a small lake a few miles northeast of Tacoma. Driving toward town each morning I drop down a hill into the broad terminal valley of the Puyallup River, which merges with the tidelands of Commencement Bay beyond which stretches the sound. On clear days the white bulwark of the Olympics hangs like a stage drop between the sound and the Pacific, while to the east Mount Rainier—we of Tacoma invariably think of it as *the* mountain—rises white and huge and separate from the forested Cascades on which the hieroglyphics of logging roads and logged-over areas can be read by the sophisticated foresters at a distance of some forty miles. With perpetual snow to the east and west, a countryside full of lakes, the mountain slopes rutted by swift streams, and the sea in the forest opening out into the great ocean, pleasure-seeking Northwest-erners often wait to the last minute and let the weather decide whether their recreation for the week end will be sailing or clamming, a ride on a ferry boat or a glide on skis, swimming or hiking, steelheading on some stream or mooch-ing for salmon from an outboard, or combing the ocean beach for storm-offered flotsam and jetsam.

To me the gray-green waters of Puget Sound have the most persistent appeal. They may reflect other colors—blue under the clear August sky, a sulphurous yellow bruised with purple as the equinoctial storms gather and break, pink or salmon in the sunset, pale green at dawn, milky brown where the glacial streams release their freight of silt, pewter under the morning mists of fall. But their essential color is gray-green.

When I think of the sound the scene most likely to come to mind is of gray-green water reaching to gray beach, of low, smooth waves opaque under a high overcast, the surface flecked by iodine kelp streaming with the current, of bluffs topped by dark evergreens and a distant shaft of sunlight impaling a hunting tern. There are, in my sound, beauty and isolation and mystery.

The beauty and the isolation persist. Not even the first sunny holiday week end of summer can dispell the mysterious essence. I recall a Memorial Day on a friend's cruiser in Pleasant Harbor on Hood Canal. Boats lay gunnel to gunnel, thick as barnacles on beachrock. Outboards whined and commuter seaplanes came down to mast-height. On every deck friends shared stories and liquor. It was a bacchanal afloat, a day when any fool (and plenty there were) had only to sound his whistle to touch off a cacophonous concert of toots and beeps and yawps. Yet when the sun disappeared behind the second growth and the last dinghy was tethered to its mother boat, isolation and beauty flooded back with the tide. In the crowded harbor could be heard faintly the wind whistling on the wings of the night birds, the splat of salmon breaking water, the creaking of oarlocks as someone went quietly about his business.

Few sounds are as evocative as those drifting across water at night. What can an oarsmen be about? Smuggler, fisherman, pilot, lover, bootlegger, log pirate? Friend or foe? The scrape of wood against iron, the drip of runoff from the blades, the hiss of water against a hull: these are sounds that snag the attention, that send the imagination probing into the coves of local history.

For those who prefer their water with stronger additives, the Northwest offers perhaps the world's more diverse assortment of aquatic races. In an area where nearly everyone has boats, boat races are as natural as rain. Before the white man came, Indians used to race their long dugouts in intervillage contests, and they still do, though usually at white men's celebrations. Tugboats once raced out to meet the sailing vessels waiting tow in the strait, and this has metamorphosed into formal races between Seattle, Tacoma, and Vancouver tugs at such occasions as Seattle's Seafair. There are rowboat races down white-water rivers in Oregon; whaleboat races between teams of Coastguardsmen; and a giddy variety of outboard contests, the wildest a stampede down the Sammamish Slough which attracts hundreds of entries. Sailboat races may start as far away as Alaska and last a week. Powerboat operators have devised the estimated-time race, in which skippers predict the length of time it will take their boats to cover a complicated course at a given engine speed, then run it without recourse to clock or change of power, and win on the basis of the accuracy of their estimates: perhaps the world's least thrilling sport for spectators, though not without its devotees. If two chips are floating down a stream, Northwesterns will pause to see which goes around the bend first.

For nearly a quarter of a century, the University of Washington's eight-oared shells dominated intercollegiate rowing as completely as Notre Dame dominated football in the same era. The Washington-California regatta on Lake Washington every other year was *the* major sporting event, drawing crowds estimated at more than a hundred thousand.

Ted Jones designed a radical hydroplane for automobile-dealer Stanley Sayres shortly after World War II; called Slo-Mo-Shun IV, it proved a winner, leaving the rest of the entries in the Gold Cup awash under the clouds of spray it kicked up on the Detroit River. The Northwest abruptly found itself in love with the unlimited hydros with their plumed roostertails, their feed-time snarls, their delicate mechanical innards.

The Gold Cup champion each year defends his title on a course of his own choosing. Stanley Sayres chose Lake Washington. Unbelievably large crowds — estimated at upwards of a quarter million by delighted publicists and outraged owners of lake-shore property — turned out to watch the Seattle boats attempt to beat back the challenge of entries from Detroit and other "eastern" cities. The rare victories by out-of-state entries were looked on as conspiracies more outrageous than Pearl Harbor, and are remembered with more rancor.

During the 1950s all other activities slowed down as the Gold Cup race drew near. It didn't matter that most hydroplane races are parades with the boat that manages to win the dash to the first turn in each heat staying in front, mile after similar mile, unless its motor falters or its hull disintegrates; nor did it matter that scoring is so complicated that it often took longer for officials to decide the winner than it had to run the two-day race — indeed some decisions have had a gestation period of months and have been delivered by officials who weren't present during the conception of the argument. It does not even matter that with the possible exception of the marathon and the fifty-thousand-meter walk no sporting event is more remote from most spectators much of the time. Everyone had to be in the vicinity when the hydroplanes were on the lake. As Gold Cup time approached fans who didn't know how to release the hoods on their autos began to talk knowingly of quillshafts and carburation. Since the main uncertainty in a Gold Cup race is which boats will break down, the phrase "dead in the water" became a regional cliché, over-worked to the point where one television station lured listeners with promises that none of its sportscasters would utter the words. The most adept of the hydro-pilots, Bill Muncey, a baby-faced daredevil with a history of being in-volved in controversial finishes, became a local folk hero and a successful disk jockey.

The peak of hydroplane hysteria appears to have passed, but the big hydros remain a part of the Northwest way of life, like high climbers and geoducks.

What baseball was to Brooklyn, sports fishing is to the Northwest. Not everyone imbibes the spirit of the pastime, but those who do are saturated with its lore and weighted with its paraphernalia. The manufacture and sale of boats and gear helps shore up the economy; on the other hand, the sportsmen's lobbies in the state legislatures provide greater obstacles to hydroelectric dams than do the uncertainties of geology and the bond market.

Salmon, steelhead, and trout are the main quarry, each with its devoted coterie of pursuers. Though there are constant complaints of the decrease of fish, particularly salmon, no corresponding diminution has occurred among fishermen. On opening day for lake fishing you can walk from one shore to the other on the more popular lakes without stepping out of rowboats; when the steelhead are running, fishermen may be elbow to elbow along the banks. Thousands of boats take to the water during the annual salmon derbies, when prizes of automobiles, television sets, and cash in thousand-dollar chunks are awarded for the heaviest fish boated. Yet even when they are cheek by jowl with their neighbors, the fishermen are away from it all, each enclosed in a little world that encompasses the angler, a circle of water out from the line, and the mystery and hope of what is going on just below the surface.

The skiers, too, are solitary in crowds as they glide down the powdered slopes of the main ski areas, which lie only a one- or two-hour drive from the major cities.

Most solitary of all are the mountaineers, the hikers, and the climbers, who follow the streams to their sources, who cross the glaciers and the snowfields to the summits they have chosen. Thoughtful people, some of them; plodders, others; but all willing to match muscle and skill and intelligence against the implacable challenge of the peaks.

The land lies lovely under the warm wet winds of the Pacific. Its cities offer delights, its waters sport, and the wilderness a place where, in the words of John Muir, "the galling harness of civilization drops off, and the wounds heal ere we are aware."

Map of

The NORTHWEST CORNER

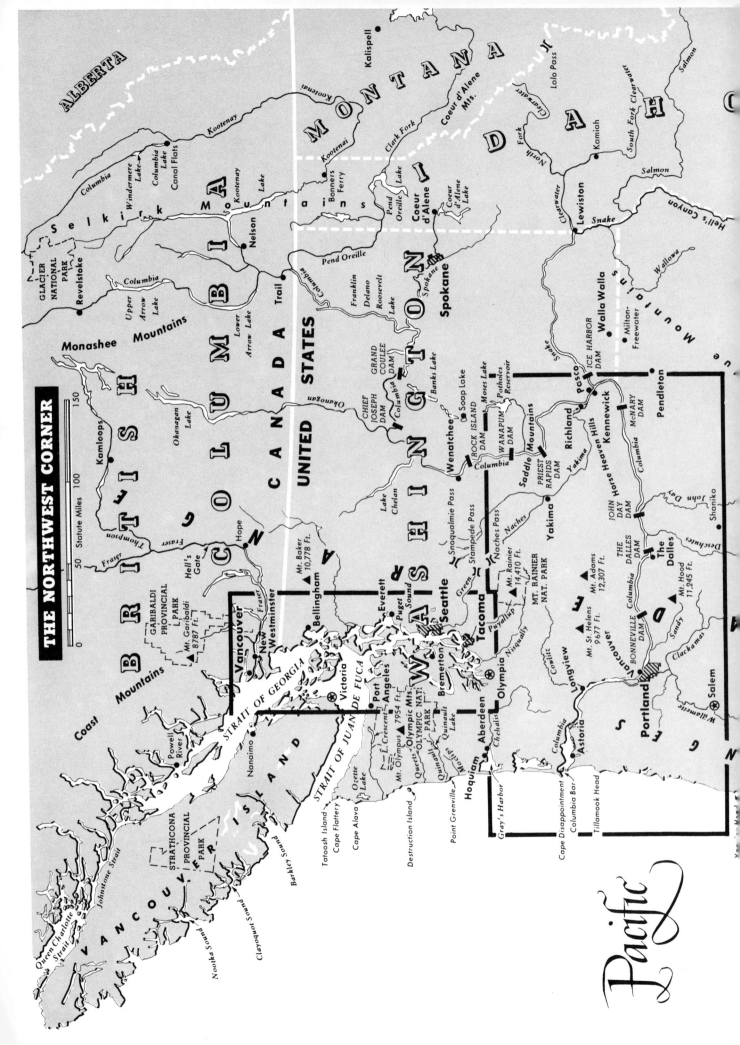

THE NORTHWEST CORNER

Statute Miles
0   50   100   150

ALBERTA

BRITISH COLUMBIA

Glacier National Park
Revelstoke
Selkirk Mountains
Columbia Lake
Windermere Lake
Canal Flats
Columbia
Kootenay
Upper Arrow Lake
Lower Arrow Lake
Monashee Mountains
Nelson
Trail
Kamloops
Okanagan Lake
Thompson
Fraser
Hope
Hell's Gate
Garibaldi Provincial Park
Mt. Garibaldi 8787 Ft.
Coast Mountains
Powell River
Vancouver
New Westminster
Nanaimo
Victoria
Strathcona Provincial Park
VANCOUVER ISLAND
Queen Charlotte Strait
Johnstone Strait
Nootka Sound
Clayoquot Sound
Barkley Sound

MONTANA
Kalispell
Kootenai
Kootenai
Clark Fork
Coeur d'Alene Mts.
Lolo Pass
Clearwater
South Fork Clearwater
Salmon
Kamiah
North Fork
IDAHO
Bonners Ferry
Pend Oreille Lake
Coeur d'Alene
Coeur d'Alene Lake
Lewiston
Snake
Hell's Canyon
Wallowa
Salmon

WASHINGTON
Pend Oreille
Spokane
Franklin Delano Roosevelt Lake
Grand Coulee Dam
Chief Joseph Dam
Columbia Dam
Banks Lake
Okanogan
Soap Lake
Moses Lake
Potholes Reservoir
Wenatchee
Rock Island Dam
Wanapum Dam
Columbia
Saddle Mountains
Priest Rapids Dam
Lake Chelan
Richland
Kennewick
Pasco
Ice Harbor Dam
Walla Walla
Milton-Freewater
Pendleton
Blue Mountains
Mt. Baker 10,778 Ft.
Bellingham
Everett
Seattle
Puget Sound
Snoqualmie Pass
Stampede Pass
Green
Naches Pass
Naches
Yakima
Yakima
John Day Dam
McNary Dam
Horse Heaven Hills
Columbia
John Day
Shaniko
Deschutes
Tacoma
Bremerton
Olympia
Puyallup
Nisqually
Mt. Rainier 14,410 Ft.
Mt. Rainier Nat. Park
Mt. Adams 12,307 Ft.
Mt. St. Helens 9,677 Ft.
The Dalles Dam
The Dalles
Mt. Hood 11,245 Ft.
Bonneville Dam
Sandy
Clackamas
Vancouver
Portland
Salem
Willamette
OREGON
Longview
Cowlitz
Astoria
Columbia
Cape Disappointment
Columbia Bar
Tillamook Head
Gray's Harbor
Hoquiam
Aberdeen
Chehalis
Point Grenville
Destruction Island
Cape Alava
Cape Flattery
Tatoosh Island
Ozette Lake
Mt. Olympus 7954 Ft.
Olympic Mts.
Olympic Nat'l Park
Queets
Quinault
Quinault Lake
Moclips
Port Angeles
Crescent L.
Strait of Juan de Fuca
Strait of Georgia

CANADA
UNITED STATES

Pacific

N

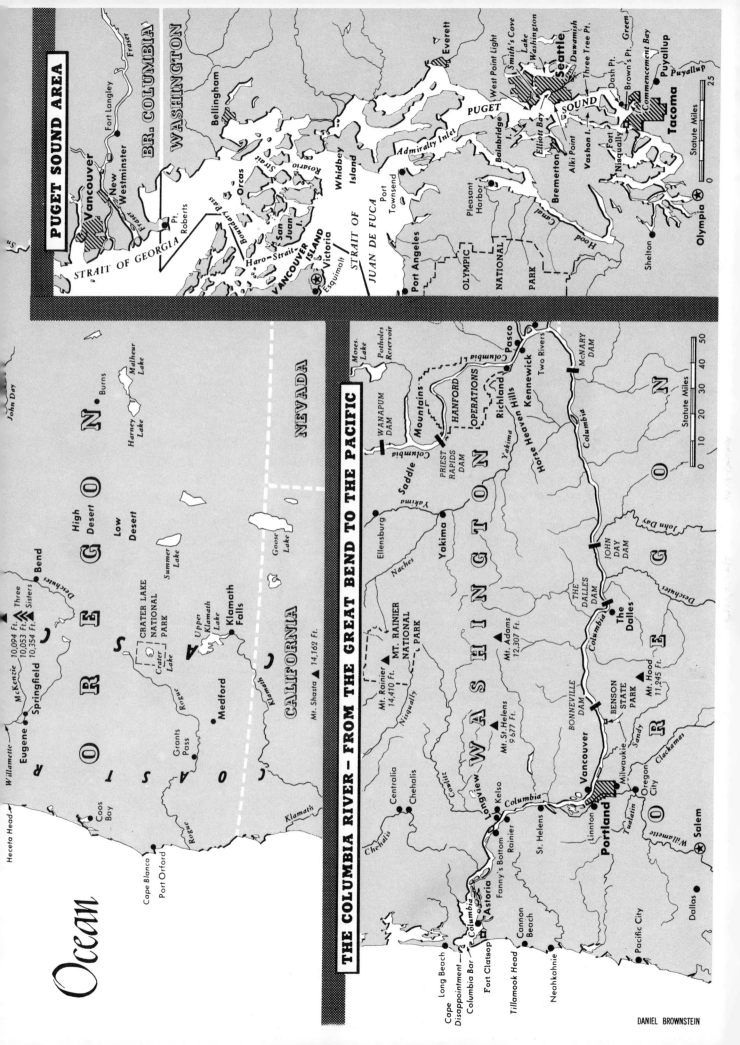

PUGET SOUND AREA

BRITISH COLUMBIA
WASHINGTON

Fraser
Fort Langley
Vancouver
New Westminster
Fraser
Pt. Roberts
Boundary Pass
STRAIT OF GEORGIA
Orcas
San Juan I.
VANCOUVER ISLAND
Victoria
Esquimalt
Haro Strait
Rosario Strait
Whidbey Island
Bellingham

Everett
Smith's Cove
Lake Washington
West Point Light
Seattle
Green
Brown's Pt.
Three Tree Pt.
Dash Pt.
Puyallup
PUGET
SOUND
Bainbridge
Elliott Bay
Alki Point
Vashon I.
Duwamish
Commencement Bay
Tacoma
Puyallup
Admiralty Inlet
Port Townsend
Port Angeles
STRAIT OF JUAN DE FUCA
Pleasant Harbor
Bremerton
Fort Nisqually
Hood Canal
OLYMPIC NATIONAL PARK
Shelton
Olympia

Statute Miles
0   25

THE COLUMBIA RIVER – FROM THE GREAT BEND TO THE PACIFIC

Ocean

John Day
Burns
Malheur Lake
Harney Lake
OREGON
High Desert
Low Desert
Summer Lake
Goose Lake
NEVADA

Three Sisters 10,094 Ft. 10,053 Ft. 10,354 Ft.
McKenzie
Springfield
Eugene
Bend
Deschutes
Willamette
CRATER LAKE NATIONAL PARK
Crater Lake
Upper Klamath Lake
Klamath Lake
Klamath Falls
Medford
Grants Pass
Rogue
Klamath
CALIFORNIA
Mt. Shasta 14,162 Ft.

Heceta Head
Coos Bay
Cape Blanco
Port Orford

Moses Lake
Potholes Reservoir
WANAPUM DAM
Columbia
Saddle Mountains
PRIEST RAPIDS DAM
HANFORD OPERATIONS
Columbia
Pasco
Richland
Kennewick
Horse Heaven Hills
Yakima
Two Rivers
McNARY DAM
Columbia
John Day
JOHN DAY DAM
WASHINGTON
Ellensburg
Naches
Yakima
Yakima
Mt. Rainier 14,410 Ft.
MT. RAINIER NATIONAL PARK
Nisqually
Mt. Adams 12,307 Ft.
THE DALLES DAM
The Dalles
Deschutes
OREGON
Mt. Hood 11,245 Ft.
BENSON STATE PARK
BONNEVILLE DAM
Columbia
Sandy
Milwaukie
Oregon City
Clackamas
Mt. St. Helens 9,677 Ft.
Centralia
Chehalis
Cowlitz
Chehalis
Longview
Kelso
Columbia
Vancouver
Portland
Linnton
Tualatin
Willamette
Salem
Dallas

Cape Disappointment
Columbia Bar
Long Beach
Fort Clatsop
Astoria
Columbia
Fanny's Bottom
Rainier
St. Helens
Tillamook Head
Neahkahnie
Cannon Beach
Pacific City

Statute Miles
0 10 20 30 40 50

DANIEL BROWNSTEIN

Index

Page references in italics refer to illustrations.